Crisis music

MANCHESTER
1824
Manchester University Press

Crisis music

The cultural politics of Rock Against Racism

Ian Goodyer

Manchester University Press
Manchester and New York

distributed in the United States exclusively by Palgrave Macmillan

The right of Ian Goodyer to be identified as the author of this work has been asserted
by him in accordance with the Copyright, Designs and Patents Act 1988.

Published by Manchester University Press
Oxford Road, Manchester M13 9NR, UK
and Room 400, 175 Fifth Avenue, New York, NY 10010, USA
www.manchesteruniversitypress.co.uk

Distributed in the United States exclusively by
Palgrave Macmillan, 175 Fifth Avenue, New York,
NY 10010, USA

Distributed in Canada exclusively by
UBC Press, University of British Columbia, 2029 West Mall,
Vancouver, BC, Canada V6T 1Z2

British Library Cataloguing-in-Publication Data
A catalogue record for this book is available from the British Library

Library of Congress Cataloging-in-Publication Data applied for

ISBN 978 0 7190 7924 5 hardback

First published 2009

18 17 16 15 14 13 12 11 10 09   10 9 8 7 6 5 4 3 2 1

Typeset by SNP Best-set Typesetter Ltd, Hong Kong
Printed in Great Britain by
CPI Antony Rowe, Chippenham, Wiltshire

For Georgina, Lily, Gabriel and, of course, Jake.

Contents

List of illustrations

Preface

This book has grown from research I originally conducted for a Master's Degree in Imperialism and Culture. The subject of Rock Against Racism (RAR) proved attractive for a number of reasons. Purely pragmatically, RAR supplied an interesting and relatively neglected area of study and hence one which provided ample opportunities for original research. It soon became apparent, furthermore, that many of those connected with RAR in the 1970s were willing to share their knowledge and experience, and I benefited enormously from their generosity.

But there are personal reasons, too, for my choice of subject. I am lucky enough to have been a teenager during the 1970s, a period when politics and music became inextricably entangled – most notably through the medium of punk rock – and I first began seriously to question the political verities with which many of my generation had become familiar. I came to punk not principally as a disaffected music fan (although I loathed the 'prog rock' I was too timid to denounce to my Rick-Wakeman-admiring peers), but as a somewhat belated convert to the joys of rock music and teen rebellion. Punk helped me to look beyond a cultural agenda still dominated in many respects by the tastes and habits of my parents' generation and it provided a context within which I could experiment more openly with novel forms of expression. And so, like many others, I began to tramp the highways and byways of the punk circuit, often travelling long distances to attend gigs. But besides my enthusiasm for this new music, I was also beguiled by the promise of sampling unfamiliar and enticing lifestyles that lay outside the experiential event horizon of my council estate in Birmingham. Along the way I met many luminaries of the punk and new wave scenes, sported an Anti-Nazi League badge, argued fiercely about the politics of race and class, and pogoed alongside my fellow iconoclasts. This present study, therefore, shares a historical space with my teenage self, even if the voice has aged 30-odd years.

As I researched RAR another reason emerged for writing this book, and it is one that applies to any investigation into the theory and practice of mass social movements. All too often the supposedly disinterested stance of scholarly investigation masks an antipathy towards the seemingly *ad hoc* and – what may seem for some – intellectually unsatisfying, business of grassroots political activism. Having been engaged in various forms of political activity over a number of years, I often felt that the lively, creative and sophisticated campaigns in which I was involved formed a sharp contrast with the rather arid works of analysis and theory that attempted to make sense of them for a less committed audience. This may be because the milieu within which political activists operate is not one that is altogether congenial to the pristine and delicately wrought ideals of the professional intellectual. But these ideals can be fragile things, which seem robust enough in the carefully tended environment of the academic seminar and learned journal, but are easily damaged by exposure to the less carefully contrived conditions of workplaces, street protests, passionate public meetings, and all those other sites familiar to the politically engaged campaigner. I am reminded of Marx's critique of idealist philosophy (to which I will return later), in which he notes that, 'in contradistinction to materialism, the active side was developed abstractly by idealism – which, of course, does not know real, sensuous activity as such.' This is not an anti-intellectual position, but rather one which recognises that any political project intending to change the world, rather than simply interpret it, needs to be rooted in lived reality.

Reading histories of RAR: some issues to consider

Oppositional groups lack the programmatic clarity of political parties and any account of them needs to recognise the contradictions built into such bodies. The diffuse coalition of individuals and organisations who assemble under a particular banner can do so for any number of reasons and their aims may spring from individual concerns or the policy objectives of a co-ordinated political tendency. This mode of operation can lend a peculiar volatility to the affairs of a protest movement, since its participants may agree on the central aim of the campaign, but little else. The fierce ideological currents that flow through and around these foci of struggle affect all those involved, whether as activists or apparently disinterested observers. This is certainly the case with RAR, where the fallout from polemical disputes is particularly evident, because so many of those who were closely involved are still very active, culturally, critically and politically. The vigorous, and frequently contentious, proceedings of campaigns such as RAR may offend the sensibilities of those for whom theoretical purity alone is the hall-mark of political success.

Difficulties of definition and analysis are often troublesome, but they are compounded in the case of RAR because the organisation operated across the heavily contested terrain of 'racial' and cultural politics. If concepts such as 'race', nation, fascism and culture are contentious, then so too is any attempt to mobilise them in the service of a particular cause. The available literature on RAR is rather scant, given the politically and culturally promiscuous nature of the movement, but even so it is still possible to discern recurrent themes that deserve comment and analysis. It is also apparent, however, that important features of the RAR phe-nomenon remain somewhat obscure. The nature of the campaign's links with the left and its place within a much wider tradition of radical cul-tural politics deserve particular consideration. Besides material dealing specifically with RAR, the organisation is encountered tangentially in a number of works on related subjects, such as the punk rock subculture, and these raise important issues for anyone working in this area.

A further difficulty in studying RAR arises from the fact that, like many similar campaigns, it operated largely informally and has not left behind the kind of 'paper trail' that more administratively rigorous organisations generate. RAR produced countless leaflets, flyers, posters, badges, newsletters, photographs and so on, but its activities were not mediated through the dissemination of policy documents, confer-ence resolutions, internal bulletins, minutes of meetings and the like. The relative dearth of this bureaucratic paraphernalia confirms the fluid and dynamic nature of RAR's decision-making processes, but it can also make it harder to gain, at a distance, a convincing picture of the movement's 'state of mind'. One of the largest archives of RAR docu-ments was destroyed in a fire, but I have benefited from access to a number of personal collections. I have also consulted records on RAR deposited with the Modern Records Centre at The University of Warwick, which are generally found within holdings relating to the Socialist Workers Party and other left-wing groups. References to these papers and documents are indicated in the following manner: IS Internal Bulletin, April 1974, pg 10, *Alistair Mutch Papers*, Modern Records Centre, University of Warwick, MSS.284. At the time of writing none of the collections I consulted has been fully catalogued; the accession number at the end of each citation therefore indicates a collection, rather than an individual document. References to the archive of book reviews held by Chatto & Windus, the publishers of *Beating Time* (David Widgery's history of RAR and the Anti-Nazi League) are labelled 'Chatto & Windus Reviews: 1986'.

Acknowledgements

This book has undergone an unusually lengthy period of gestation. It started out in 2000, with an attempt to think of a viable subject for an MA dissertation, and eight years later it has finally grown wings (or at least a spine). For their support and advice during this time certain people deserve a special mention. All those who agreed to be interviewed, and who are cited in the text, were crucial to the project, and I thank them. Certain people, however, were exceptionally generous with their time and expertise. Syd Shelton, Ruth Gregory, Red Saunders, Roger Huddle and Ian Birchall not only submitted themselves to my questioning, but also responded to my numerous emails and requests with remarkable alacrity and patience. Red, Syd, Ian and Roger all read versions of the manuscript and offered useful suggestions and corrections. Dave Renton, John Street and Seth Hague encouraged me to seek a publisher for my dissertation, and John very kindly gave me access to research and papers from the University of East Anglia's 'Striking A Chord' project. Roger Sabin contributed to a lengthy and spirited correspondence during which we agreed to disagree on many things, but in a remarkably amicable fashion. The staff at Warwick University's Modern Records Centre were tremendously helpful in tracking down obscure material scattered throughout their archives. Chatto & Windus kindly supplied copies of all the reviews they hold of David Widgery's book *Beating Time*. Some sections of this present work are based on my earlier article, 'Rock Against Racism: Multiculturalism and political mobilization 1976–81', which was published in *Immigrants and Minorities* (2003) vol. 22, no. 1; I thank Taylor & Francis (www.informaworld.com) for granting me permission to reuse parts of this text.

The history and politics of Rock Against Racism still provoke wide-ranging debates and disagreements and any contribution to the literature is bound to attract its share of criticism, so it is especially important for me to apply the standard caveat regarding the author's sole responsibility for all interpretations, errors and omissions in this book.

Finally, Georgina, Lily and Gabriel have been a constant source of encouragement, and have had to put up with my lengthy and selfish absences from domestic life during the writing process. I really don't know what I have done to deserve such a family.

List of abbreviations

AFC	anti-fascist committee
ANL	Anti-Nazi League
BNP	British National Party
CAST	Cartoon Archetypal Slogan Theatre
CP	British Communist Party
FI	Fourth International
FN	Front National
IS	International Socialists
LMHR	Love Music Hate Racism
MFS	Music for Socialism
NAFF	National Association for Freedom
NF	National Front
NME	*New Musical Express*
NRFM	National Rank and File Movement
RAC	Rock Against Communism
RAR	Rock Against Racism
RTWC	Right To Work Campaign
SWP	Socialist Workers Party
UAF	Unite Against Fascism
UEA	University of East Anglia
WMA	Workers' Music Association
YNF	Young National Front

Introduction

Rock Against Racism operated between 1976 and 1981,[1] and was a mass campaign that combined anti-racist politics with popular culture. Throughout this period RAR used the medium of concerts featuring black and white musicians as a focus for, and practical demonstration of, its politics of 'inter-racial' unity. The campaign's most significant political sponsor was the Socialist Workers Party (SWP), a small but influential organisation of revolutionary socialists who, as we shall see, espoused (and still do) a non-orthodox version of Trotskyism. One consequence of the party's political outlook, I will argue, was that it fostered a more tolerant attitude on the part of some members towards popular culture in general, and rock music in particular, than was typical of most of the British left. However, a particular interpretation of Marxist theory was only one element in the willingness of key SWP activists to break ranks with the left's traditional disdain for 'mass culture'. The path to RAR was far more circuitous than this suggests, passing via the counter-cultural struggles of the 1960s and the explosion of modernist cultural experimentation in the early twentieth century. But besides this debt to older antecedents, RAR seized on contemporary developments in popular culture, including the two musical forms that became most closely identified with RAR: punk rock and reggae.

After spending a lengthy period in relative obscurity, RAR's leading role in the anti-racist mobilisations of the 1970s has become more widely recognised in recent years. Dave Renton's history of the Anti-Nazi League (ANL), *When We Touched the Sky*,[2] Alan Miles's documentary film, *Who Shot the Sheriff?*,[3] and the work of the Striking A Chord project at the University of East Anglia (UEA), have all helped to revive interest in a movement that clearly prefigured later developments in the fields of pop and politics. The only book-length treatment of the subject to date remains David Widgery's *Beating Time*, which provides a vivid and politically engaged eyewitness account of the movement.[4] It is, however, long out of print and in any case does not attempt the kind of theoretical overview that this present study attempts. Paul Gilroy's discussion of RAR in *There Ain't No Black In The Union Jack* offers a sympathetic and insightful analysis of the campaign's cultural politics, although it has little to say about RAR's origins, or the left-wing milieu from which the organisation emerged.[5] These works are discussed below, as are numerous other commentaries and critiques, but it is clear that there has been little attempt so far to clarify the political and organisational forms that inspired RAR, or to relate the movement to other attempts by the left to enlist popular culture in various social struggles. It must also be noted that the ethnic and cultural parameters of popular music have changed significantly since many appraisals of RAR were written, changing irrevocably the foundations upon which it was based.

The story of RAR is part of a complicated, and still controversial, period in British history. The collapse of the post-war consensus and the ascent of neo-liberalism are still shaping the way we live, and the experience of RAR demonstrates that the passage from the mid-1970s to the present has not been either frictionless or uncontested. But RAR is more than a mere historical curiosity, for the movement seems to prefigure some of the preoccupations and interests of a new generation of young activists, who have risen up around the world in protest against such issues as capitalist globalisation, the threat of ecological catastrophe, and resurgent tendencies towards war and militarism. Some of the cultural and political means through which contemporary youth demonstrate their discontents bear a family resemblance to those employed by RAR between 1976 and 1981. With this in mind, we might like to consider how RAR either anticipates or contrasts with present-day manifestations of 'celebrity' and 'lifestyle' politics. Even if we confine ourselves to the realm of popular music, it is possible to cite numerous examples of campaigns that are organised around the idea of celebrity endorsement of 'good causes'. Some of these occupy similar territory to RAR, but each has its own social dynamic and political trajectory.

It is tempting to see only the novelty in RAR; to regard it as an unequivocal break with the dour worthiness of the 'old left'. This perception has been encouraged to some extent by RAR's supporters, who have been keen to stress the critical distance between themselves and a left-wing milieu which typically rejected any accommodation with the products of 'Americanised' popular culture. Whilst this view contains strong elements of truth, we must also appreciate that RAR was not totally unprecedented. It was a movement with a distinct lineage, and it drew inspiration from various cultural and political precursors, including early twentieth-century cultural avant-gardes, some of which would find favour with many an old leftist.

One of my aims is to locate RAR within a lengthy tradition of left-wing engagement with popular culture; a tradition which, by the mid-1970s, had imbibed some of the spirit of the so-called 'New Left' – a political tendency which was in itself a reaction against both the stultifying dogmatism of official Communism and the patently reactionary nature of Stalinism. But RAR could trace its break with the dull 'routinism' of the labour movement to a point before the emergence of the New Left, when a crisis within the Trotskyist Fourth International (FI) led one small section to abandon its illusions in the progressive nature of Stalinised 'workers' states', but, unlike the New Left, without forsaking its allegiance to the principles of Bolshevism.[6] This rejection of key tenets of 'orthodox' Trotskyism implied, amongst other things, a refusal to automatically privilege the cultural products of 'state capitalist' regimes over the often more beguiling creations of their unashamedly capitalist rivals – particularly the USA.

The creation of a space within which a revolutionary, anti-Stalinist, politics could flourish provided an important corrective to the unreflective pro-Kremlin line of official British Communism, but I will argue that it was the changing fortunes of the British class struggle in the 1970s which prompted important elements on the left to embrace the potential of cultural activism, and consequently to establish RAR. The decline in previously high levels of rank and file industrial militancy, combined with the increasing threat from the National Front (NF), made socialists more receptive to forms of struggle that appealed to constituencies outside of the workplace. The activists who founded RAR were therefore not simply pursuing their own enthusiasms, they were also – consciously or not – compensating for the lack of a powerful industrial challenge to racism and fascism.

Besides defining RAR's relationship with the British left, I also want to suggest how the organisation developed a cultural politics that accepted the necessity of engaging with the products of the capitalist 'culture industry', without succumbing to the pacifying effects of what Marxists term 'commodity fetishism'. To elucidate my arguments I will draw on comparisons between RAR and other significant politico-cultural movements, principally the post-war folk revival, which arose in opposition to the spread of commercialised 'mass culture', and Bob Geldof's various 'Aid' initiatives, which embraced this culture wholeheartedly.

But if RAR needs to be understood within the context of a broader left-wing current in British politics, we also need to grasp the extent to which it forged links with, and relied upon, wider networks of influence and talent. These included concerned individuals, cultural bodies, political organisations, performers, music venues and the press. Recent scholarship has started to map these links and it is becoming increasingly apparent that it was RAR's ability to assemble and motivate a broad and willing coalition of disparate allies that allowed it to extend its reach so fast and so far. I will argue that RAR's success in building such a powerful presence was not simply a result of pragmatic bridge building, but was, instead, deeply influenced by political theories that can trace their origins to the early twentieth century, and the search for strategic perspectives for socialists internationally in the wake of the Russian revolution. In particular, many RAR activists were guided by the example of the united front, which, although it was imperfectly realised in Rock Against Racism, gained fuller expression with the founding of the Anti-Nazi League.

It is inevitable that a movement as adventurous and ambitious as RAR should excite controversy, and there are a number of specific criticisms that I wish to explore in depth. One that still generates considerable comment is RAR's relatively narrow cultural foundations – preeminently punk rock and reggae – and the various ethnic exclusions that such a bias implies. This has been addressed in several recent studies, and a number of critics have drawn attention to the apparently marginal position of Asian people within RAR's project. In its severest form this criticism extends to the accusation that RAR turned its back on Asian victims of racism and adopted an elitist and implicitly racist position typical of the so-called 'white left'. Gaining a clear perspective on this debate demands that we re-examine the reasons behind RAR's musical 'policy' and appreciate in particular the role played by reggae as both a bridge between white and black youth and as a symbol of the resistance of Afro-Caribbean people to oppression at the hands of the British state.

If cultural exclusivity within RAR draws the fire of some critics, then the organisation's determination to tap the energy of punk rock draws fire from another direction. Some commentators contend that RAR's intervention in punk represented a conservative influence, which inhibited punks from freely exploring the radical potential inherent in their repertoire of shocking and spectacular modes of behaviour and display. RAR's critical response to such practices as the wearing of Nazi insignia was, according to this view, just the most visible example of the campaign's failure to appreciate the 'ironic' and subversive intentions behind punks' attitudes. My aim is not simply to revisit a well rehearsed debate, but to examine some of the motives and assumptions that underlie the argument, and to situate it within the context of the far-right's struggle to build an identity that could appeal to disaffected white youth. I also question some widely accepted beliefs regarding the cultural and political bases of punk rock, and in the process I criticise the ways in which certain readings of the movement exaggerate the influence of highly visible and articulate elites that did not reflect the reality of punk beyond the purlieus of the Kings Road and Soho.

A note on 'race'

Before proceeding I would like to make a point about terminology. The words 'race', 'racism' and other words and terms denoting 'racial' categories occur frequently throughout this book and it is useful to take a moment to clarify how such slippery concepts are being used. I am in agreement with those writers who regard race as a social, and not a biological, construct; as a 'category shaped by social beliefs and perceptions'.[7] It has often been the case that those most committed to a racialised view of humanity have striven to identify characteristics, most notably skin colour and physiognomy, which could be used to signify racial divisions between peoples. What is evident, however, is that even these distinguishing features vary widely within racial groups, thus making distinctions between races impossible to establish unequivocally. In any case, whatever superficial distinctions we can observe between geographically dispersed peoples, it has become clear that these traits occur on the basis of a remarkable degree of uniformity between human beings in terms of their genetic make-up, with the bulk of diversity occurring within, rather than between, races. In Richard Dawkins' words: 'If all humans were wiped out except one local race, the great majority of the genetic variation in the human species would be preserved.'[8]

But if race is an invalid concept at the biological level, it has acquired considerable ideological significance for reasons to do with relations of oppression and exploitation established over several centuries. It is the innate connection between racism and socio-economic relations which informs Peter Alexander's definition of racism as 'a particular form of oppression: discrimination against people on the grounds that some inherited characteristic, for example colour, makes them inferior to their oppressors.'[9] The ideological (in the sense of being a product of 'false consciousness') nature of race-thinking might lead one to conclude that we should not flatter racism by acknowledging it as a serious subject of study, or focus of resistance. This is, I believe, a mistake. I concur, rather, with James Donald and Ali Rattansi, who make the following point: 'Reiterating that "there's no such thing as 'race'" offers only the frail reassurance that there *shouldn't* be a problem. It cannot deal with the problems that do exist, because it fails to see them for what they are.'[10] As Donald and Rattansi make clear, though, many modern racists take aim not at the biological inferiority of non-white races, but at the undesirability of their cultural practices. Speaking in 1978, the Conservative Party leader and future Prime Minister Margaret Thatcher managed to invoke three articles of the racist creed – colour, culture and immigration – when she spoke about limiting the numbers of people entering Britain from, in particular, the New Commonwealth and Pakistan. During a TV interview Thatcher declared that 'people are really rather afraid that this country might be rather swamped by people with a different culture'.[11]

The shift away from the pseudo-scientific concept of race and towards the more culture-bound notion of 'ethnicity' – at least in terms of public discourse – represents, in part, a retreat by racists to a more defensible position. Elaborate taxonomic hierarchies based on such phenotypical features as eye shape, skeletal structure and skin colour have had enormous ideological significance, especially during the heyday of imperialism, but the essential dishonesty of white supremacism, and of its bogusly empirical 'scientific' foundations, was evident even at the height of colonial slavery. Slaves were useful to their masters, after all, not because they were subhuman, but because they were rational beings, or as Robin Blackburn puts it, 'men and women capable of understanding and executing complex orders, and of intricate co-operative techniques'.[12] As Blackburn goes on to explain, this vital truth lies behind the insecurity of the slave-owner's own position: 'The most disturbing thing about the slaves from the slaveholder's point of view was not cultural difference but the basic similarity between himself and his property.'

The peculiar mix of arrogance and fear that defines racism as an ideological position, even until today, is thus prefigured in the mind-set of early colonists:

> The American planter who treated his slaves like subhumans would typically reveal a fear and surplus aggression towards them which stemmed from a belief that they could take over his plantation and his womenfolk if they were given the slightest real opportunity to do so.[13]

Of course times change and racism has evolved many forms. The brutal inequities typical of slave-based societies were not always supportable or appropriate to the needs of imperial powers, and, as in the British Raj, imperialism often depended on the collusion of local proxies, all of whom had their own ambitions to satisfy. The assumption of racial superiority on the part of the colonial authorities did not disappear in these cases, but it might find itself articulated through paternalist doctrines which stressed the civilising mission of imperialism.[14] From this point of

view the empire's subjects were not so much goods and chattels to be
bought and sold (or, as was the case with so many indigenous peoples,
vermin, to be exterminated), they were, rather, children, who needed
guidance and discipline from their white mothers and fathers.[15]

But we are concerned with Britain in the 1970s: a place and time
where the multiple legacies of an imperial past became entangled with
messy realities of economic distress. These circumstances revived racist
ideas in a particularly virulent form. Gone were the days when British
economic and military power gave its ruling class the self-assurance to
either disregard the aspirations of subject peoples, or to dispense the
largesse necessary to ensure their ascent to the status of true civilisation.
Not only was Britain much reduced in economic terms, but the orbit
within which its power held sway had become consequently smaller.
Even in the British Isles themselves the resumed 'troubles' in Ireland
exerted a corrosive influence on the self-confidence of British nationalists. And as Britain's reach became ever more restricted, so did the
mental landscape of the country's racist fringe. On the far-right, race
hatred was no longer a confident expression of Britain's international
ambitions, but a defensive retreat into sullen insularity. But the dream
of inhabiting a racially homogeneous homeland was thwarted by the
presence of large numbers of black and Asian citizens and by the threat,
as racists saw it, of grasping immigrants, eager to leech resources from
their economically enfeebled host. The fears experienced by the American planter had thus found a new setting, for now the hate figures did
not populate colonial plantations far from the imperial centre, but the
towns and cities of the motherland itself. Racists therefore vented their
paranoid despair through invocations against the country being
'swamped' by migrant workers and alien cultures, and in doing so both
their language and their actions became increasingly intemperate and
even violent. In such conditions a fascist party like the National Front
could revive a political project based on identifying and attacking ethnic
and racial minorities and all those who would defend a multicultural
society.

A further note on terminology

For the sake of convenience I have followed certain conventions
throughout this book in referring to ethnic minority communities. In
Britain the word 'Asian', when applied to people, generally denotes
those who can trace their recent ancestry to south Asia, and more
specifically the Indian sub-continent, and this is the sense in which I use
it. Likewise, 'black' typically refers to people who can claim African

descent, and I have used the word in the same way. Because much of the discussion concerns communities hailing from the West Indies I have also used the terms West Indian, Afro-Caribbean and Anglo-Caribbean synonymously. Needless to say, I acknowledge the crudity and inadequacy of such vocabulary and rely upon the sagacity of the reader in accepting these conventions for the rough approximations to reality that they represent.

Notes

1 The last of the large-scale RAR carnivals was held in July 1981, although small local groups continued operating after this date. Hull RAR was active until 1982. See: www.hullrockagainstracism.co.uk/posters.htm.
2 Dave Renton, *When We Touched the Sky: The Anti-Nazi League 1977–1981* (New Clarion Press, London, 2006).
3 Alan Miles, *Who Shot The Sheriff? Riot, race, rock and roll – Rock Against Racism 1976–1981* (Mad Inertia Productions Ltd, London, 2008).
4 David Widgery, *Beating Time: Riot 'n' race 'n' rock 'n' roll* (Chatto and Windus, London, 1986).
5 Paul Gilroy, *There Ain't No Black in the Union Jack: The cultural politics of race and nation* (Routledge, London 1992).
6 The idea of establishing an organisation to coordinate the activities of the international workers' movement is as old as Marxism itself. The First International, associated with Marx and Engels themselves, was wound up in the 1870s, following the defeat of the Paris Commune and the decreasing effectiveness of the organisation. The Second International (or the Socialist International as it is often called) was founded in 1889 by the leaders of the mass social democratic parties that had developed in various countries – the largest and most successful of these being the German SPD. This body was succeeded by the Third International (the Communist International, or Comintern as it became known), which was founded in 1919 following the revolution in Russia and the revolutionary upsurge that gripped Europe after the First World War. The Second International had previously demonstrated its inability to act as a stimulus to revolution when, in 1914, most of its member parties sided with their 'own' ruling classes on the outbreak of war. The eventual 'Stalinisation' of the Comintern, and its conversion into a tool of Russian foreign policy, led the exiled revolutionary leader Leon Trotsky to declare the foundation of a Fourth International in 1938. See: August H. Nimtz, Jr, *Marx and Engels: Their contribution to the democratic breakthrough* (State University of New York Press, Albany, 2000), chs 7–9; Marcel Liebman, *Leninism Under Lenin* (Merlin Press, London, 1980), part IV, ch. 3; Alex Callinicos, *Trotskyism* (Open University Press, Milton Keynes, 1990), pp. 17–49; Marxists Internet Archive, www.marxists.org.

7 Robert Miles and Annie Phizacklea, 'Some introductory observations on race and politics in Britain', in Robert Miles and Annie Phizacklea (eds), *Racism and Political Action in Britain* (Routledge & Kegan Paul, London, 1979), p. 2.

8 Richard Dawkins, *The Ancestor's Tale: A pilgrimage to the dawn of life* (Weidenfeld & Nicolson, London, 2004), p. 336. See also: Steven Rose, R.C. Lewontin and Leon J. Kamin, *Not In Our Genes: Biology, ideology and human nature* (Penguin, Harmondsworth, 1984), pp. 119–127; Mark Ridley, *Evolution*, 3rd edition (Blackwell, Oxford, 2004), pp. 374–377.

9 Peter Alexander, *Racism, Resistance and Revolution* (Bookmarks, London, 1987), p. 5.

10 From the introduction to James Donald and Ali Rattansi (eds), *'Race', Culture and Difference* (Sage Publications Ltd in association with Open University Press, London, 1992), p. 1.

11 www.margaretthatcher.org, downloaded 25 October 2007. See also Alex Callinicos, *Race and Class* (Bookmarks, London, 1993), p. 32.

12 Robin Blackburn, *The Making of New World Slavery: From the baroque to the modern 1492–1800* (Verso, London, 1997), p. 12.

13 Blackburn, *New World Slavery*, pp. 12–13.

14 A.P. Thornton, *Doctrines of Imperialism* (John Wiley & Sons Ltd, London, 1965), ch 4.

15 This outlook is nowhere better exemplified than in the works of psychologist J.C. Carothers: 'The peculiarities of primitive African thinking can for the most part be well explained on the assumption that "phantastic" thinking plays a larger part in it than "directed" thinking. "Phantastic" thinking, as defined by Jung, is characteristic of day-dreams, dreams and myths, is especially marked in children and primitive peoples and is essentially an immature mode of thought.' J.C. Carothers, 'A study of the mental derangement of Africans, and an attempt to explain its peculiarities, more especially in relation to the African attitude to life', *Journal of Mental Science* (1947), p. 592.

1

Origins and contexts

As I noted in the introduction to this book, Rock Against Racism was a mass anti-racist movement that used rock concerts as a medium through which to organise resistance to the British far-right. It is a striking irony, therefore, that RAR – an organisation dedicated to multicultural ideals – was stirred into life by a racist outburst from Eric Clapton, a white musician whose whole career was, after all, built on the basis of a profound respect for black music such as reggae and rhythm 'n' blues. Nevertheless, when he addressed the audience between songs at an August 1976 gig at the Birmingham Odeon, Clapton chose as his theme the perils of black immigration and the political wisdom of that notorious enemy of multiculturalism, the MP Enoch Powell. Many people were struck by the incongruity of such sentiments being expressed by a man made rich through interpreting and performing blues and reggae, but the writer Caryl Phillips, who as a schoolboy attended the fateful gig with white friends, experienced Clapton's outburst on a deeply personal level. In Robin Denselow's book, *When the Music's Over*, Phillips recalls his shock and bewilderment at Clapton's assertion that, 'Enoch was right – I think we should send them all back', and his demand to 'Keep Britain white'. Phillips recalls that he went to the concert to hear 'about as black a musician as I ever listened to',[1] but what he actually discovered was that skill in articulating black cultural idioms did not insulate musicians either from wider social influences, or the alienating effects of a music industry that exploited the commercial potential of black music without necessarily acknowledging the contributions of those artists who originally inspired people like Clapton.[2]

Eric Clapton's words would have excited controversy at any time, but in 1976, in Britain, he was touching nerves already rubbed raw by an increasingly abrasive wave of intolerance and bigotry. Rock star David Bowie's remarks about Britain's need for a fascist dictator, and the Nazi salute with which he greeted British fans[3] were indicative of a worrying trend, but beyond the histrionic fantasies of the 'thin white duke' racial tensions were being ratcheted up by the National Front, a fascist party which was becoming an increasingly credible electoral force, as well as an intimidating presence on the streets. Amidst a generalised attack on immigration in the national press, much of it aimed at the arrival of Malawi Asians in May 1976, the NF fielded dozens of candidates in local elections, gaining around 18.5 per cent of the vote in Leicester and 10 per cent in Bradford. Worrying, too, was the combined 44 per cent share of the vote taken by the NF and the National Party in a 1976 council by-election in the south London constituency of Deptford.[4]

The growing threat of the NF was not lost on Red Saunders, a London-based photographer and veteran political activist, who responded to Clapton's outburst with an angry letter to the music press, which was co-signed by a number of like-minded friends and political associates. The spectacle of one of Britain's most eminent blues musicians making common cause with racists and parochial English nationalists prompted Saunders and his co-signatories to write: 'Own up, half your music is black. You are rock music's biggest colonist. You're a good musician but where would you be without the blues and R&B?'[5]

But registering a protest against one man's hypocrisy was not the main purpose of the letter, which went on to call for the formation of a 'rank and file movement against the racist poison in rock music'.[6] This summons to action met with an enthusiastic response, with over 600 replies being received in the fortnight following the letter's insertions in the music press, and hundreds more following its publication in the SWP's weekly paper, *Socialist Worker*. Seizing the initiative, RAR's founders began organising concerts at which black and white bands shared the stage in public displays of multicultural unity. Further afield, the initial contacts made through Saunders' letter provided the basis for a national movement which, between 1976 and 1981, operated on an ambitious scale. In 1978 alone RAR organised 300 local gigs and five carnivals, including two enormous London events run jointly with the Anti-Nazi League.[7] In the run-up to the 1979 general election it staged a 'Militant Entertainment Tour', which featured around 40 bands at 23 concerts, and covered some '2,000 miles on the road'.[8] RAR could also claim the support of many of the most innovative musical acts of the time, including the Tom Robinson Band, Sham 69, Steel Pulse, Aswad, the Members, X-Ray Spex, Stiff Little Fingers, the Specials and the Clash. Through its slogan, 'Reggae, Soul, Rock and Roll, Jazz, Funk and Punk: Our Music',[9] RAR declared its intention to deny popular music to the forces of the far-right, but although a multiplicity of styles were represented at their events it is clear from the concert line-ups that punk, 'new wave' and reggae were the mainstays of RAR's musical offer.[10]

From the start RAR had close links to the SWP; a number of key figures, such as Roger Huddle and David Widgery, being party members and others, like Red Saunders, being close to the organisation.[11] The willingness of the SWP to underwrite RAR is evident in the party's provision of office facilities for the fledgling movement; the address given for correspondence in the founding letter was the SWP's National Office in Cottons Gardens, in London.[12] Although RAR maintained a small headquarters[13] the bulk of the movement's supporters were dispersed throughout the UK in local groups, which numbered 60–70 in 1979.[14] The members of this disparate network exercised considerable autonomy,[15] but one of the channels through which they communicated and organised was RAR's journal, *Temporary Hoarding*. This magazine ran for 14 issues between 1977 and 1981, and it carried practical guidance for local organisers, concert reviews and timetables, interviews, posters, letters, reportage and political articles. RAR also produced regular circulars and gig guides for its supporters[16] and a stream of propaganda and publicity material in the form of badges, leaflets, stickers, t-shirts, posters, postcards and placards, as well as graphic backdrops for concerts. A compilation album, *RAR's Greatest Hits*, was released on Virgin Records and a video and slide show was also produced, for use at concerts and discos.[17]

One of RAR's most distinctive features was its strong visual identity, which drew heavily upon the art and graphics of early twentieth-century radical cultures, but was also influenced by punk graphics, pop art and the availability of new printing technologies. The typographic style of the campaign's literature and stage graphics betrays the influence of Dada and the Russian designer Aleksandr Rodchenko. The format of *Temporary Hoarding* was directly inspired by Russian revolutionary wall newspapers, whilst the use of montage is redolent of John Heartfield and even Robert Rauschenberg. The campaign's logo, a five-pointed star, is a direct echo of socialist iconography.[18] Even RAR's (and the ANL's) distinctive circular 'lollipop' placards were apparently derived from old photographs of Russian demonstrations.[19]

RAR's supporters claim that, as part of a wider anti-racist and anti-fascist current, the movement contributed to the demise of the NF as a serious electoral and political force. Furthermore, they insist that RAR promoted an ethos within popular music that heralded a more multicultural scene in later years. Along the way attitudes towards popular culture among the revolutionary left were transformed, from cynicism to constructive engagement.

All political movements bear the marks of their birth and of course RAR is no exception. The campaign arose during a period that could seem, to those who had grown up in a post-war bubble of prosperity and optimism, to be filled with ill omens and grim portents. This was a time when many of the social and material props of the so-called post-war consensus crumbled away; in particular there was a growing perception that Keynesian economics had failed to deliver on its promise of economic stability. But other symptoms of this malaise also became manifest, such as sharpening racial tensions, the rise and fall of a militant rank-and-file movement in the working class, increasing social and political polarisation, and the emergence of significant youth subcultures with, occasionally, radical agendas. If we are to understand RAR we will need to acquaint ourselves more fully with these contextual issues.

The decline of consensus

Between 1945 and the mid-1970s British governance was informed by a widely held set of assumptions regarding economic management and social policy. Martin Pugh identifies five main strands to this consensus: the maintenance of full (or near-full) employment, a commitment to the welfare state, the conviction that Britain should operate a mixed economy, a belief that trade unions deserved a role in formulating government policy, and broad agreement over foreign and defence matters.[20] On the domestic front this informal framework represented not so much a drive to eradicate sources of social antagonisms as an attempt to keep them in check; this much is evident in Tory MP Quintin Hogg's warning to the House of Commons in 1943 that, 'if you do not give the people social reform, they are going to give you social revolution'.[21] Tensions within the political establishment were evident even before the war was over, with arguments over the role and extent of state intervention and over the scope and nature of the new National Health Service, for instance.[22] In some sectors, education for example, the post-war settlement can even be argued to have entrenched certain forms of inequality.[23] We should, therefore, approach the idea of consensus cautiously and in the knowledge that it describes certain broad trends within the British polity, rather than a period of social and ideological harmony.

The collapse of consensus in the 1970s was hastened by economic and ideological crises that shattered many people's dreams of progress and prosperity and the Keynesian world view upon which they were based.[24] Up until this point a degree of complacency regarding Britain's social and economic prospects was evident in certain quarters. Many young people, for instance, will have been ill-prepared for the realities of life by reading these words, which conclude a standard work on Keynes studied by thousands of A-Level economics students:

> Whatever the qualifications, the basic fact is that with the acceptance of
> the *General Theory*, the days of uncontrollable mass unemployment in
> advanced industrial countries are over. Other economic problems may
> threaten; this one, at least, has passed into history.[25]

This sanguine assessment was shaken from 1973 onwards, as a global
economic downturn undercut Britain's ability to sustain the policies that
had helped maintain post-war social cohesion. Although the economic
crisis was a global phenomenon, Britain's exposure to it was particularly
severe and the country struggled under the burden of high levels of
inflation and unemployment, combined with low levels of economic
growth – or 'stagflation' as it came to be known. The extent and gravity
of the British experience in the 1970s was evident across the board:
'The case for a severe economic downturn in the early 1970s is clear;
the decline in economic performance in that decade was manifest in key
indicators of activity, such as GDP per head, unemployment, inflation
and productivity.'[26] This led, according to one account, to 'the severest
setback to output relative to the previous trend rate of growth of any
peacetime period since 1850'.[27] By 1977 mass unemployment beckoned
and the punk rock band, the Clash, sang bitterly about 'Career opportunities, the ones that never knock'. Many of the generation who gave
us punk will have lived their childhoods in the expectation of increasing
affluence and security, but they were approaching adulthood with a
growing sense of unease. It is hardly surprising that for lots of young
people the collapse of consensus could appear as more than a mere
misfortune; it could also feel like a betrayal.

The monetarist challenge to Keynesian orthodoxy, which was to
provide one of the central ideological thrusts behind Thatcherite Con-
servatism, was rehearsed under the 1974–79 Labour government. Faced
with the International Monetary Fund's demands for reductions in
British public expenditure, Prime Minister James Callaghan and others
urged a package of spending cuts, rather than 'pump priming' (strategi-
cally deployed increases in public spending), as the answer to the post-
1973 economic downturn. 1976 was the year in which the Labour
Party's new leader declared, 'You cannot now, if you ever could, spend
your way out of a recession'.[28]

A 'social contract' (or social con-trick, to its detractors), underwritten
by the leaderships of the trade union movement and the Labour Party,
was meant to forestall antagonisms between workers and government,[29]
but it came to grief when an extended period of pay restraint failed to
secure the social reforms and economic stability that underpinned the
government's end of the deal. Relations between the two sides remained

fragile and in 1978–79 the so-called 'winter of discontent' saw a wave of strikes that hastened the demise of the government. This crisis marked a point where economic crisis and increasing social polarisation finally put paid to the post-war consensus and ushered in 18 years of Conservative government.[30]

Many on the left were angered and bewildered by the experience of Labour in office, and within the Labour Party some backed Tony Benn as a figurehead for a hoped-for radical revival.[31] Within the unions the social contract, which had been promulgated and negotiated through the official machinery of the movement, had succeeded in bypassing and marginalising the rank and file structures through which much of the left had been operating and which had played an important part in bringing down the Heath government in 1974. Those socialists who had aligned themselves with this movement were left severely disoriented as a result.[32]

The politics of despair

Leon Trotsky's dictum that 'fascism is the politics of counter-revolutionary despair' captures one of its most salient characteristics. Parties such as the NF thrive in conditions where economic and social crises are confronted by organs of working-class resistance, such as trade unions, which have become demoralised or confused. The failure of the Wilson/ Callaghan government to live up to its promises, whilst simultaneously drawing the teeth of the union rank and file, opened up a space within which NF demagogues like Martin Webster and John Tyndall could peddle solutions based on alternative forms of solidarity in the shape of race and nation.[33]

The growing confidence of the NF could be discerned in its tactic of staging provocative marches through areas with significant ethnic minority populations, often under the banner of saving white citizens from the depredations of lawless immigrants. The party's preoccupation with crime, and its demands to clamp down on left-wing subversion, echoed the sentiments of many right-wingers who saw a spell of disciplinarian government as an antidote to national decline and working-class militancy.[34]

The NF, however, needs to be situated within a wider nationalist discourse; one which had been shaped by Britain's experience as an imperial, and post-imperial, power. The far-right's attempts to articulate a coherent sense of national identity had to come to terms with Britain's post-war disengagement from Empire – a process which was marked by profound ideological convulsions. The reconstitution of the British

Empire as a Commonwealth may have helped to ease some of the distress accompanying Britain's loss of status, but it was a transformation that confirmed the straitened circumstances in which the country now found itself.[35] As A.P. Thornton argues, any attempt to 'defend the Empire against the surging tides of colonial nationalism' would have required greater reserves of men, money and materiel than Great Britain could either spend or borrow. In any case, the hostility of the USA to any such attempt would have guaranteed its failure.[36] But the Second World War entailed more than a major shift in the global balance of power; it also represented an enormous blow to European intellectual and cultural prestige:

> The major justification of the imperialist doctrine of civilization had been that imperial control opened up for a subject race greater possibilities of life: wider horizons, the blessings of a superior culture, a world filled not only with better mousetraps but with higher thought. This argument could not make sense to the educated among the subject races, as they assessed the results of this new civil war that their masters had indulged in. Embarrassed memories of African fetish and *juju* paled before a thunderstruck confrontation of gas chambers and genocide. The glamour of the European image faded in the fiercer glow of high-explosive bombs on London and on Hamburg; while the atomic bomb, dropped on Japanese cities, served only to prove to Asians and to Africans that 'the west' thought that there were some things too dangerous to be used in a civil war, yet which well might be experimented with in areas that *Herrenvolk* deemed less important to the continuance of civilization.[37]

The imperial idea, then, had suffered irreparable damage, but its replacement, in Britain's case, by the more equitable concept of a Commonwealth also brought problems. Some people were eager for Britain (and more specifically, England) to discard completely its links with its former Empire, for any concession to the notion that the 'mother country' still had a leading role to play in the affairs of formerly subject nations implied a continuation of imperial obligations towards these same nations as well; this included a duty to allow citizens of the Commonwealth the right to settle in Britain.[38] Enoch Powell, one of the most influential voices on the British right, charted a course from (in Paul Foot's phrase) 'Grand Imperialist to Little Englander' and came to see the Commonwealth as a 'disastrous encumbrance from which Britain must break free'.[39] In a speech delivered on St George's Day in 1961, Powell took the opportunity to propose an alternative nationalist philosophy in which the experience of Empire was subsumed into a long-term, essentialist narrative of English nationhood. As Powell expressed it:

Thus our generation is one which comes home again from years of distant wandering. We discover affinities with earlier generations of English, generations before the 'expansion of England', who felt no country but this to be their own. We look upon the traces which they left with a new curiosity, the curiosity of finding ourselves once more akin with the old English.[40]

This mystical evocation of the English spirit bore a strong resemblance to the Nazi concept of the national community (*Volksgemeinschaft*)[41] and it was consistent with the belief that England should maintain high levels of racial and cultural purity.[42] But such a self-conscious retreat from formerly expansive ideas of Britain's place in the world represented a withdrawal of the, often grudging, welcome given to immigrants from the Commonwealth, who were lauded initially as productive workers, emigrating in response to labour shortages in British industry.[43]

It is telling that Enoch Powell, a man who had done so much to promote the anti-immigrant sentiments upon which the NF thrived, should spring to Eric Clapton's mind during his outburst in Birmingham. During the 1970s the tightly circumscribed nationalist perspectives of the British far-right merged with a worsening economic crisis at home and abroad to create a sense of desperation upon which reactionary politics could feed. Such circumstances, however, could stimulate a variety of political and cultural responses. In the field of youth culture the anger, frustration and ennui felt by many young people in this period found a voice in forms such as punk rock and reggae.[44] Punk, however, was a markedly ambivalent cultural phenomenon, which could accommodate diverse political stances. The use of Nazi insignia within the genre's symbolic repertoire signalled a determination, on the part of some punks, to accept no restraints on their desire to experiment with 'shocking' modes of expression. Whether intended or not, such attitudes helped to define a subcultural milieu in which fascist ideas hoped to find an audience. Many bands took pains to disassociate themselves from the far-right, but the new music scene provided a context within which organisations like the NF and British Movement could begin to operate and 'white power' rhetoric could enter the punk idiom. A notorious example of this tendency is the band Skrewdriver, a punk rock outfit that became increasingly fascistic, until eventually forming part of the pro-Nazi 'Blood and Honour' music movement.[45] As we shall see, though, those who promoted the politics of race and nation did not necessarily receive a ready welcome in the subcultures they attempted to influence.

Notes

1 Robin Denselow, *When the Music's Over: The story of political pop* (Faber and Faber, London, 1989), p. 139. There are numerous references elsewhere to Clapton's infamous remarks, including: Franklin Bruno, *Armed Forces* (Continuum, New York, 2005), pp. 38–39; Luke Bainbridge, *The Ten Right-Wing Rockers*, http://observer.guardian.co.uk/print/0,,330925087–111639,00.html, downloaded 4 December 2007.

2 Even today, Eric Clapton has difficulty in constructing a convincing rationale for his remarks. Despite (according to various sources) his use of phrases such as 'Keep Britain white' and 'Send the wogs back', he insists these were 'never meant to be a racial statement'. Rather, he claims he was motivated by concerns over the government's line on immigration: 'It was more of an attack on that government's policies on cheap labour, and the cultural confusion and overcrowding that resulted from what was clearly a greed-based policy.' Descending from his attempt to scale the moral high ground, however, Clapton appeals to a mixture of masculine pride and xenophobia when he complains that another factor in the situation was that 'Pattie [Clapton's wife] had just been leered at by a member of the Saudi royal family'. See: Eric Clapton with Christopher Simon Sykes, *Eric Clapton: The Autobiography* (Century, London, 2007), pp. 99–100.

3 Jon Savage, *England's Dreaming: Sex Pistols and punk rock* (Faber and Faber, London, 1992), pp. 242–243.

4 Nigel Copsey, *Anti-Fascism in Britain* (Macmillan, London, 2000), p. 123; Gareth Jenkins, 'The badge of prejudice', *Socialist Review*, No. 234 (October 1999).

5 *New Musical Express* (11 September 1976), p. 50.

6 Ibid.

7 *Temporary Hoarding*, No. 8 (March/April 1979), p. 2; Widgery, *Beating Time*, pp. 79–101.

8 *Temporary Hoarding*, No. 8 (March/April 1979), p. 6.

9 Widgery, *Beating Time*, p. 53.

10 There are difficulties in quantifying this precisely, since not only are the genres in question not rigidly defined, but the gig reviews in RAR's journal, *Temporary Hoarding*, do not necessarily indicate the style of music performed by particular acts. It may be the case that local RAR groups staged a more eclectic mix of performers than the larger, centrally organised events, but, even so, where the nature of the performers is clarified a reggae/punk/new wave slant is apparent. The interviews that *Temporary Hoarding* conducted with musicians also betray the bias I have suggested. My interviews with RAR activists tend to confirm the idea of a musical bias. It is the case that the organisation did try to broaden its appeal at various points and to live more fully up to its slogan, especially as the radical promise of punk rock declined: see 'Back to RAR roots', *Temporary Hoarding*, No. 6 (Summer 1978); 'RAR. NAT. DUB. CON. NO. ONE.' [RAR National Dub Conference Number One], *Temporary Hoarding*, No. 7 (Winter 1979).

Despite these attempts, however, RAR maintained the focus that I (and others) have identified.

11 Red Saunders and Roger Huddle, interview (4 June 2000).

12 Red Saunders, personal communication (15 August 2001).

13 Roger Huddle, personal communication (11 December 2000); Syd Shelton and Ruth Gregory, interview (16 May 2001).

14 *Temporary Hoarding*, No. 7 (Winter 1979), p. 22.

15 Simon Frith and John Street, 'Rock Against Racism and Red Wedge: From music to politics, from politics to music', in Reebee Garofalo (ed.), *Rockin' the Boat: Mass music and mass movements* (South End Press, Boston MA, 1992), p. 70; Red Saunders and Roger Huddle, interview (4 June 2000).

16 'Back to RAR roots', *Temporary Hoarding*, No. 6 (Summer 1978).

17 RAR merchandise was promoted through *Temporary Hoarding*. I compiled this list from issues No. 5 (Spring 1978); No. 6 (Summer 1978); No. 11 (January/February 1980); No. 12 (1980); No. 14 (August 1981).

18 There was a debate over RAR's use of the red star, principally because of its association with Stalinist Communism. There is insufficient space here to develop this discussion further, but it was revived in Roger Sabin (ed.), *Punk Rock: So What? The cultural legacy of punk* (Routledge, London, 1999), p. 207. Roger Huddle has acknowledged that the star may be tainted to some extent by its association with Stalinism, but notes that RAR's use of the device represents a direct symbolic link to those anti-fascists who opposed it to the swastika in the inter-war years. As he also points out, the star was not always red, but 'appeared in a rainbow of colours'. Roger Huddle, personal communications (11 December 2000 and 12 December 2000).

19 Red Saunders and Roger Huddle, interview (4 June 2000); Syd Shelton and Ruth Gregory, interview (16 May 2001).

20 Martin Pugh, *State and Society: British political & social history 1870–1992* (Edward Arnold, London, 1994), p. 243.

21 Cited in Gregg Philo (ed.), *Glasgow Media Group Reader, Volume 2: Industry, economy war and politics* (Routledge, London, 1995), p. 199.

22 David Childs, *Britain Since 1945: A political history* (Routledge, London, 1997), ch 2; Edward Royle, *Modern Britain: A social history 1750–1997* (Arnold, London, 1997), pp. 208–213; Peter Clarke, *Hope and Glory: Britain 1900–1990* (Penguin, London, 1996), ch 7; Pugh, *State and Society*, pp. 229–245.

23 Kenneth O. Morgan, *The People's Peace: British history since 1945* (Oxford University Press, Oxford, 1999), ch 1.

24 Michael Stewart, *Keynes and After* (Penguin, Middlesex, 1972), chs 8–11. For a wider discussion of the notion of a Keynesian 'revolution' see Kerry Schott, 'The rise of Keynesian economics: Britain 1940–64', in David Held et al (eds), *States & Societies* (Basil Blackwell, Oxford, 1985), ch 4.3. Some of the expectations and problems experienced between 1945 and the 1970s are discussed in Janet Roebuck, *The Making of Modern English Society*

from 1850 (Victorian & Modern History Book Club, Newton Abbot, 1974), ch 8. We should note that there were many commentators who drew attention to the drawbacks to the 'affluent society', e.g. Guy Debord, *The Society of the Spectacle*, http://library.nothingness.org/articles/SI/en/display/16, downloaded 7 November 2007; E.J. Mishan, *The Costs of Economic Growth* (Penguin, Middlesex, 1969).

25 Stewart, *Keynes*, p. 299.

26 Roger Lloyd-Jones and M.J. Lewis, *British Industrial Capitalism Since the Industrial Revolution* (UCL Press, London, 1998), p. 186.

27 Sean Glynn and Alan Booth, *Modern Britain: An economic and social history* (Routledge, London, 1996) pp. 193–194.

28 Kenneth O. Morgan, *The People's Peace*, p. 382.

29 Anthony Sampson, *The Changing Anatomy of Britain* (Hodder and Stoughton, London, 1982), pp. 56–57; Tony Cliff and Donny Gluckstein, *The Labour Party: A Marxist history* (Bookmarks, London, 1988), p. 331; Clarke, *Hope and Glory*, pp. 317–318.

30 Cliff and Gluckstein, *The Labour Party*, ch 15. There are many analyses of the crisis in Keynesianism and the roots of the economic crisis of the 1970s, for example: Francis Green and Bob Sutcliffe, *The Profit System: The economics of capitalism* (Penguin, Middlesex, 1987), chs 15 and 16; Chris Harman, *Explaining the Crisis: A Marxist re-appraisal* (Bookmarks, London, 1984), ch 3; Lloyd-Jones and Lewis, *British Industrial Capitalism*, chs 8 and 9; Charles More, *The Industrial Age: Economy & society in Britain 1750–1985* (Longman, Essex, 1989), ch 26.

31 Sampson, *Changing Anatomy*, pp. 81–95. For a taste of the Bennite agenda see Tony Benn, *Arguments for Socialism*, edited by Chris Mullin (Jonathan Cape, London, 1979), ch 2.

32 Tony Cliff, *A World To Win: Life of a revolutionary* (Bookmarks, London, 2000), chs 6 and 7; Tony Cliff, 'The balance of class forces in recent years', *International Socialism Journal*, 2:6 (Autumn 1979). The disillusionment of many socialists provoked a debate about the proper relationship between the Labour Party and the workers' movement as a whole, e.g. George Bridges, 'The Communist Party and the struggle for hegemony'; Duncan Hallas, 'How can we move on?'; Peter Jenkins, 'The Labour Party and the politics of transition'; Ralph Milliband, 'The future of socialism in England'; all in *Socialist Register* (1977).

33 Martin Walker, *The National Front* (Fontana, Glasgow, 1977), chs 7 and 8; Caroline Coon, 'The man who would be fuehrer' [sic], *Sounds* (25 March 1978), pp. 30–32.

34 Some of the features of this militaristic solution had already been rehearsed during the war in Northern Ireland and the establishment of the strike-breaking apparatus of the Civil Contingencies Unit. Morgan, *People's Peace*, p. 388.

35 Paul B. Rich, *Prospero's Return? Historical essays on race, culture and British society* (Hansib, London, 1994), ch 1.

36 A.P. Thornton, *Doctrines of Imperialism* (John Wiley & Sons, London, 1965), ch 5.
37 Thornton, *Doctrines of Imperialism*, p. 209.
38 This right became codified in 'The British Nationality Act' of 1948. See: Paul Foot, *The Rise of Enoch Powell* (Penguin, Middlesex, 1969), ch 1.
39 Foot, *Enoch Powell*, p. 30.
40 Cited in: Simon Heffer, *Like the Roman: The life of Enoch Powell* (Weidenfeld & Nicolson, London, 1998), p. 337. Powell's emerging focus on England, rather than Empire, is described in Foot, *Enoch Powell*, ch 1. See also the discussions in A.J. Davies, *We, the Nation: The Conservative Party and the pursuit of power* (Abacus, London, 1996), ch 14; and Paul B. Rich, 'British imperial decline and the forging of English patriotic memory, 1918–1980', in Rich, *Prospero's Return?*.
41 Ian Kershaw, *Hitler 1889–1936: Hubris* (Penguin, London, 1998), pp. 134–139.
42 Richard Thurlow, *Fascism in Britain: A history, 1918–1985* (Basil Blackwell, Oxford, 1987), chs 11 and 12.
43 Paul Foot, *Immigration and Race in British Politics* (Penguin, Middlesex, 1965), chs 1, 7 and 8.
44 Savage, *England's Dreaming*, pp. 107–122; Lloyd Bradley, *Bass Culture: When reggae was king* (Viking, London, 2000), ch 18.
45 Roger Sabin, ' "I won't let that dago by": rethinking punk and racism', in Sabin, *Punk Rock: So What?*; Stewart Home, *Cranked Up Really High: Genre theory and punk rock* (CodeX, Hove, 1995), ch 8. Thankfully, the notoriety of Skrewdriver did not translate into commercial success, and, as Home points out, lead singer Ian Stuart's dream of fame and wealth was never realised (he died in 1993).

2

Critical responses to
Rock Against Racism

Socialism and anti-racism

The most obvious place to start in assessing Rock Against Racism's politics and its links with the Socialist Workers Party is the account in David Widgery's book *Beating Time*, which provides, as yet, the most comprehensive treatment of RAR. Written from an insider's perspective (Widgery was one of RAR's leading lights and a prominent SWP intellectual), *Beating Time* advances the argument that the RAR/SWP partnership was crucial, both for the success of RAR and the health of socialism in Britain. RAR enabled socialists to express their ideas through a new cultural vernacular, one that allowed them to openly discuss and celebrate their pleasures and to create a more joyful and optimistic vision of socialism than was current on the left. Widgery's hopes for a revival of left-wing cultural enthusiasm found an echo among the SWP's membership, as is evident in this extract from *Rent-amob*, a SWP 'agitprop bulletin':

> Go to the average left-wing meeting – a speaker who may be good, but followed by a generally lifeless question-and-answer session and a list of exhortations from the chair. Yet the struggle for socialism is the struggle to tap the immense creative, imaginative ability of working people, the enthusiasm that is crushed by class society.[1]

The SWP provided vital logistical support to RAR in the shape of printing and office facilities, and this enabled the organisation to establish itself during a period of rapid initial growth, but the party also supplied many of RAR's leading cadres and, through them, it exercised a significant level of influence over the movement's politics. Crucially, the SWP also offered a political and organisational link with the Anti-Nazi League, which was another of the great anti-racist initiatives of the 1970s, but one that tapped into a different set of constituencies from RAR.

The SWP's influence can be felt at various points in RAR's politics. It shows up, for instance, in the sustained critique of capitalism that informed the organisation's anti-racism. This critical stance enabled RAR to explore and attempt to draw connections between topics such as gender and sexual politics, British imperialism, the role of the state, and the war in Ireland. One of the aspects of RAR that commended it to Paul Gilroy, despite his disavowal of Marxism, is this political breadth, which he claims distinguished it from the more narrowly focused ANL.[2] Gilroy contends that RAR attempted to address the pervasive racism that provided the bedrock of British fascism, whereas ANL propaganda tended to employ nationalistic tropes that emphasised the alien nature of the NF's politics, with specific reference to Britain's defiance of German Nazism during the Second World War. This is a theme picked up by Nigel Copsey, who, like Gilroy, draws attention to the nationalist rhetoric that some critics have detected at the heart of the League's propaganda. In harking back to Britain's wartime anti-Nazi solidarity, and mobilising this myth to expose the supposedly 'sham' patriotism of the NF, the ANL is accused of restricting the scope of anti-racist work, while simultaneously pandering to the kinds of romantic nationalism to which racists often appeal.

> League propaganda paid little attention to the popular racism in which support for the National Front was located. This was quite deliberate because the ANL rightly assumed that British public opinion would find the designation 'NF = Nazis' much more offensive than simply objecting to the Front's 'racism'. The ANL thus looked to reactivate patriotism generated by the Second World War rather than address the roots of fascism in popular ideologies of racism.[3]

But Copsey's and Gilroy's arguments have been challenged by Dave Renton, who claims they are based on a very inaccurate reading of the ANL's literature. According to Renton, the kinds of nationalistic references to which Gilroy refers are 'almost entirely absent' from ANL publications, although they do crop up in pronouncements from 'other groups . . . including sometimes the Communist Party.' He also draws attention to the ANL's involvement in broad anti-racist activities, such as the League's sponsorship of the Campaign Against Racist Laws, and the direct involvement of ANL supporters in initiatives like the day of action called in response to the New Cross fire, in which 14 black people had been killed.[4]

Gilroy's appreciation of RAR mirrors Widgery's contention that a consistent anti-racism is feasible only on the basis of a wide-ranging theoretical assault on the institutions and ideas that underpin the 'establishment'. In accordance with this principle RAR constantly pushed against the constraints of traditional anti-racist campaigning by making propaganda around the issue of oppression in general. In doing so it gave expression to the idea that oppressive practices such as sexism, homophobia and racism are social lubricants of capitalism, since they sow divisions amongst those whom the system exploits.

If the SWP, at least according to some accounts, provided much of RAR's political substance, Widgery did not believe the relationship was one-sided; he saw in RAR an opportunity to inject new life into the lacklustre routines of revolutionary socialism and to counter the moralism and the bureaucratic mentality that had plagued much of the British left. In support of this view, Widgery's account emphasises the spontaneous militancy that he sees emerging from the social conditions prevailing in crisis-bound Britain and which RAR helped to channel. As he and fellow RAR activists wrote, 'working class kids NOW are political and fun without having to make 5 minute speeches to prove it'.[5] Widgery's apparent eagerness to yield the political initiative to such radicalising influences as punk rock and angry British youth led one party critic, Ian Birchall, to claim that he saw 'everything from the standpoint of the mass movement, nothing from the standpoint of the party'.[6] According to Birchall, Widgery placed a naive faith in goodwill rather than 'hard politics',[7] and he attributes this shortcoming to Widgery's failure to develop a coherent theory of ideology. What emerges through reading *Beating Time*, claims Birchall, is a narrative that offers important insights into the process of building a mass campaign, but leaves revolutionaries none the wiser as to how to advance their politics within it. This tendency to diminish the importance of party organisation was criticised by another of Widgery's comrades in the SWP, Pat Stack, who insisted that his failure to address the limitations of cultural politics led to the impression that 'the imagination of the guardians of youth culture seems to be as important as the political groundwork'.[8]

One of the points at issue between Birchall and Widgery is how best to articulate the relationship between the revolutionary party and the working class. This is, understandably, an important debate on the far-left of the political spectrum, especially for those who, like the SWP, draw political inspiration from a Bolshevik tradition that demanded the utmost clarity on issues of organisation. For Paul Gilroy, though, this class perspective diverts us from the real significance of RAR. Gilroy contends that racial and social identities are in a constant state of tension and that they become coherent only through a process of struggle. He disputes Marxism's insistence on the primacy of class distinctions, contending, rather, that race and class are inherently unstable formations, developing out of the solidarities that arise from the working out of a multiplicity of societal antagonisms. Viewed in this light RAR provided one of the sites at which new social and ethnic relationships were being realised – a point at which the energies unleashed by social discord and political struggle could generate new structures of differentiation and identity. In some ways this agrees with Widgery's view that a vital politico-cultural dynamic can be discerned in the prosaic realities of multicultural, urban, British life, but unlike Widgery, Gilroy implies that RAR's success was achieved despite, rather than because of, its political affiliations to revolutionary socialism. Gilroy acknowledges, and applauds, the SWP's display of initiative, but he accords the party's intervention a secondary place in his analytical scheme. According to Ashley Dawson, an important precursor to RAR's organisational methods can be found in the work of C.L.R. James, who, claims Dawson, stresses the vitality and militancy of spontaneous struggles whilst rejecting the vanguardism of the revolutionary left.[9] A pronounced distrust of the SWP's motives for involvement in RAR is evident among some commentators, for whom the party's participation in anti-racist struggles must be regarded as a cynical exercise on behalf of an organisation with its own sectarian axe to grind. The SWP's orientation on anti-racism has been construed as evidence of the party's determination to exploit a popular movement for its own narrow ends,[10] with some critics maintaining that the SWP's influence was inimical to the long-term integrity of the anti-racist movement.[11] But these criticisms need to be set against the fact that the SWP's involvement in anti-racist struggles had a lengthy pedigree, and often entailed defending progressive principles in very difficult circumstances. Party members in the London docks, for instance, had taken a principled stand against Enoch Powell at a time when a significant minority of dockers struck in defence of him following his infamous 'rivers of blood' diatribe. Although we should be careful not to exaggerate the extent of Powell's active support among dock workers, SWP activists did not pursue the easy option of opportunistic silence in the face of hostility and unpopularity, but rather pursued hard arguments with co-workers who were often otherwise staunch allies in this notoriously tough and militant industry. This position can be contrasted with the equivocation of many left-wing – including British Communist Party (CP) – activists at the time, as can the SWP's rejection of the idea that the British state could be persuaded to apply immigration controls in an equitable and 'colour-blind' fashion.[12]

The precise nature and extent of the SWP's involvement in RAR is difficult to gauge, but there is strong evidence for the view that the party played a vital role in establishing and maintaining RAR, whilst ceding considerable autonomy to local initiatives. It is apparent that RAR was not expanding into a vacuum. Renton and Copsey have both noted how a widespread anti-racist and anti-fascist milieu had developed around the time of RAR's inception.[13] In part this had arisen in response to the NF's evident growth, and the threat it seemed to be assuming in electoral terms. A number of anti-fascist committees (AFCs) – sometimes set up at the instigation of trades councils and the radical left, at others by bodies such as local Race Equality Councils and the Labour Party – had been established across the country. One of the chief tasks of these AFCs was to distribute anti-NF propaganda, a task made much easier by the ready availability of research into the political backgrounds of leading NF members by the magazine *Searchlight*. But if the growing confidence and audacity of the NF provided the mood music for a period characterised by increasing racial tensions, specific campaigns and struggles helped to sharpen the left's appreciation of the multiple dimensions of the struggle they were undertaking.

The strike at Grunwick – a north London film processing plant – which began in August 1976, grew from a fight over pay and conditions and for the right to belong to a trade union. But the action, which saw a mainly Asian workforce pitted against both their employer and the police force, drew support from many quarters, including postal workers refusing to handle the company's mail, a number of Labour MPs, the Communist Party and the National Union of Mineworkers. The first mass picket of the company was bolstered by a contingent of supporters from the SWP-sponsored Right To Work Campaign (RTWC), who were celebrating the acquittal of the RTWC National Secretary, John Deason, on public order charges.[14] On the other side, the employers benefited from the assistance of the right-wing National Association for Freedom (NAFF), which had a number of links to sympathetic politicians and industrialists keen to push an anti-union agenda. NAFF, which helped to organise and fund Grunwick management's legal battle against the unions, was a fiercely anti-Communist ginger group that was also not reluctant to propagandise on behalf of racist political regimes around the world. In a period of generally low levels of working-class militancy, the Grunwick dispute, with its mass pickets and violent confrontations with authority, provided a vivid illustration of the ways in which the politics of race and class were inextricably entwined.[15] Much lower key than the strike at Grunwick, but of considerable symbolic importance, was the case of Robert Relf, a racist homeowner in Leamington, who advertised his house for sale to a 'white family' only. Relf, whose affiliations to the far-right were evident in his previous membership of organisations like the National Socialist Movement, became subject to an intense anti-racist campaign, which resulted in a successful prosecution under the Race Relations Act and the ignominy of his original 'for sale' sign being publicly burned in the largely Asian suburb of Southall in London.[16]

Numerous other marches, demonstrations and campaigns were taking place as RAR found its feet in 1976–77 and they help us locate the movement as an important, but by no means isolated, strand within a much broader anti-racist and anti-fascist crusade. These stirrings of a populist anti-racism suggest that RAR could tap into resources beyond the scope of the organisation's immediate sponsors, and research undertaken at the University of East Anglia, as part of the Striking A Chord project, confirms how RAR was often sustained, at the local level, by cultural and political networks that had grown up prior to, and independently of, RAR itself.[17] Through interviews with RAR activists in Manchester, Coventry, Leeds and London, the UEA team has revealed, for instance, that 'RAR in Manchester in 1976 was closely associated with the first Deeply Vale festival, a four to five day, free, outdoor event'. Key people associated with this festival supplied sound equipment for RAR gigs (including the Manchester carnival) and participated in RAR events as both organisers and performers. Far from the SWP, or RAR's London centre, calling all the shots in the provinces, Street, Hague and Savigny claim, 'it is evident that the networks which forged the music scene – the venues, the retailers, the local media – were instrumental in organising RAR'.[18] But Manchester was not unique in this respect. In Coventry too, according to one interviewee, a local coalition of 'lumpen intelligentsia; teachers, social workers, semi-employed, self-employed, artists, writers and musicians'[19] formed the basis of RAR. Viewed in this light, it would seem that RAR, although clearly influenced by the SWP's version of Marxism, was by no means a party fiefdom. One of the defining features of the movement, according to some accounts at least, was its ability to mobilise support outside of the SWP and the traditional structures of the left.

> In short, RAR came out of networks or scenes in which formal political organisations were only peripheral players. Couched in the language of political participation . . . RAR emerged as part of a counterpublic, organised at a local level and depending on non-mainstream media and networks.[20]

Further evidence for RAR's local roots comes from Bristol, where the Ashton Court festival was renamed in 1978 the 'Rock Against Racism/ Free Community Festival'. This combined typical elements of RAR's brand of cultural activism, such as reggae and punk music, with more 'traditional' features like 'plays, stalls, art etc', and the distinctly non-punk sounds of Steve Hillage.[21]

One of the channels through which RAR was able to express its cultural politics was the British music press, which in the mid-1970s was becoming increasingly radicalised. The major 'inkies', especially *Sounds* and the *New Musical Express* (*NME*), came under the influence of a generation of journalists and editors who were keen to explore the political ramifications of a music scene that had been profoundly affected by the arrival of punk rock.

> In the period prior to, and following RAR, some elements of the music press became more and more receptive to the idea that music and politics should be linked. Individuals like Neil Spencer, who was to become editor of the NME in 1978, increasingly politicised the coverage of music. In doing so, they encouraged their readers to see music as political and musicians as politicians.[22]

RAR events, particularly the carnivals, were given prominent coverage in the music papers, with *Sounds* offering RAR space to promote itself in the journal's special report on racism in the music industry.[23] It seems evident to some participants that RAR was not simply catching the mood of the moment, but was involved in a symbiotic relationship with music reporters and the companies they worked for. This created the conditions under which a more politically engaged music journalism could both find an audience and turn a profit. One of the organisers of Stevenage RAR declares:

> You could argue that the media played a significant role as well – every one of the organisers read the NME avidly and it had started the pressure with articles on Bowie and Clapton, but you could argue that IPC [the NME's publishers] allowed the NME to become a politicised music paper because it was so clear that influences like RAR had made it possible for NME to make money by being politicised.[24]

RAR's ability to articulate the concerns of a broad social constituency is examined in Simon Frith and John Street's essay *Rock Against Racism and Red Wedge*. Red Wedge, formed in 1986 as an anti-Thatcherite coalition between musicians and the Labour Party's electoral machine, was tied from the start to an electoral agenda. The campaign's musical support came from an eclectic range of performers, including overtly political figures such as Billy Bragg, Jerry Dammers, Tom Robinson and Paul Weller, to less radical artists like Sade and Dave Stewart. Labour's intention, which was to mobilise popular culture in an attempt to dramatise its message to young voters and to boost the party's performance at the polls, meant that Red Wedge's goals were from the start tightly constrained within a reformist framework. This perspective inevitably implied that the movement's audience would be allocated a passive role in political affairs. RAR, however, was more concerned with the transformative potential of mass culture. It strove to create an atmosphere in which participants could see beyond the present system to, perhaps, revolutionary conclusions. In both organisations musicians acted as spokespeople for youth, but whereas in Red Wedge the interests of young people were communicated to the Labour Party in order to influence its policy-making, in RAR these interests were reflected back onto the audience as a stimulus to direct action. So Red Wedge was, in Frith and Street's words 'formed by and for a political party', but RAR was 'ideologically at any rate, a spontaneous movement of musicians and fans, concerned with the politics of the everyday'.[25]

Frith and Street acknowledge the SWP as RAR's most important political backer, but they distinguish between it and the Labour Party's modes of operation. Labour kept a tight rein on Red Wedge's activities, but the SWP was less concerned with exercising direct control over RAR, preferring 'to educate and direct those involved, to provide a theory and a practice',[26] in the process of which, the party would hope to extend its influence and perhaps recruit members.

It seems to be widely accepted, then, that RAR was able to consolidate itself on the basis of political and cultural resources that were already in place by the time that Saunders et al were attempting to launch the organisation, but Robin Denselow is unwilling to give much credit to one element in this mix – punk rock – for shaping RAR's politico-cultural identity. Unlike some commentators, including Paul Gilroy and Dick Hebdige, who discern a potential for spontaneous radicalism at the subcultural level at which punk operated, Denselow regards RAR as an attempt to give a lead to fragmented and contradictory political and cultural tendencies. Denselow argues: 'Whatever else punk may have been, it was no unified scene'[27] and that a coherent and organised pop-cultural response to racism would need to be generated outside the structures of rock's old and new establishments. In Denselow's view RAR 'was a movement that would never have existed if it hadn't been for the energy, enthusiasm, and hatred of the National Front generated by members of the Socialist Workers' Party'.[28]

Roger Sabin, who edited a collection of revisionist essays on the punk phenomenon, shares Denselow's scepticism regarding the organic radicalism of punk rock. He reveals that a close examination of the genre's fans and performers shows that they were all too susceptible to the lure of the far-right. In his essay on the subject Sabin reinforces Denselow's observations about punk's political ambivalence, but he emphasises, too, a strain of racism permeating the subculture, whether it be in the form of racist song lyrics or a blindness towards the plight of those ethnic minorities who lacked the cultural cachet of Anglo-Caribbean rebel youth. He thus claims that Britain's Asians, who endured much of the far-right's violence in the 1970s, were often invisible to punk's radical vanguard and at worst were despised by them.[29] Sabin's appraisal of RAR is less sanguine than Denselow's, largely because he believes that the organisation internalised this prevailing mood through its concentration on a narrow stratum of popular-cultural forms, from which Asian music was conspicuously excluded. He also suggests that many of those white people who championed West Indian youth and reggae held attitudes that were themselves mediated through a set of racist stereotypes.[30] Sabin's views echo those of critics of naive multiculturalism, who take issue with the tendency to 'essentialise' 'host' and immigrant cultures, and thus reduce them to an assemblage of stereotypical and internally homogeneous practices and beliefs. Often characterised as the 'saris, steel-bands and samosas syndrome', this strand of multiculturalism stands accused of trivialising and over-simplifying what are in fact complicated and highly differentiated ways of life.[31] RAR's sponsorship of reggae, and the organisation's attempts to build links with West Indian youth could be construed, therefore, as a validation of prevailing cultural stereotypes concerning, on one hand, the innate rebelliousness of Afro-Caribbeans and, on the other, the passivity of Asians.

Sabin's conclusions concur with those of another group of critics, who have implicated RAR in a broad critique of the 'white left' and its role in anti-racism. They claim that a number of important bodies, such as the Indian Workers Association and the Asian Youth Movements, had been largely ignored or misunderstood by the left and they observe:

> Music and other cultural forms were central to their activities for mobilisation, commemoration and celebration. Nevertheless, the Anti-Nazi League and Rock Against Racism were unable to foster a productive relationship with these organisations. This was a result not only of the marginalization of 'race' politics by the ANL, but also of a pervasive xenophobia and nationalism in much of the British Left during this period.[32]

This criticism is reinforced by the claim that RAR was dominated by white organisers, who tended to ignore the black musicians who were also involved in the movement. The anti-Nazi political priorities of both RAR and the ANL eclipsed the concerns of these black activists and typified a tendency on the white left to 'parachute' into racial struggles, only to abandon them once their potential was exhausted.

A further problem identified by Sabin is that any organised response to racism ran the risk of repelling many of those punk rockers for whom the genre's anarchism and iconoclasm were its most appealing features. This could only be exacerbated by RAR's open identification with the revolutionary left, who were seen, in certain quarters, as politically symmetrical with fascism.[33]

Jon Savage also takes an ambivalent stance towards RAR and like Sabin his point of entry into the debate is via the medium of punk rock. Savage, however, sees in punk a source of radicalism that was bound up with its commitment to a set of controversial and confrontational attitudes and practices. These included unorthodox performing styles and the calculated display of politically loaded symbols such as the swastika. Savage notes that such a discourse translates uneasily into conventional politics or mass-market acceptability. When viewed from this perspective, RAR represents a political formation that was unable to assimilate punk's ambiguous and self-consciously shocking modes of action and representation. Savage does not discard the positive results of RAR's campaign, noting that the first carnival 'eradicated forever the miasma of fascism that still hung over Punk',[34] but he maintains that in the conflict between pragmatic dogma and utopian gesture it was the latter that came off worst. As Savage puts it:

> There had long been hostility between anarchists, believing in 'the flux of never-ending change', and the more rigid, schematic approach of Hegelians and Marxists, contradictions which had been contained within the SI [Situationist International] and Punk but which were now, under intense pressure, exposed.[35]

The view that RAR's Marxist leanings implied a simplistic approach to punk has also been suggested by Dave Laing. In describing RAR's attitude towards Sham 69 vocalist, Jimmy Pursey, who, despite his support for RAR, refused to take a judgemental attitude towards a racist element among his fans, Laing has this to say:

> RAR's own implicit position, like that of Pursey, was one of 'realism': the role of the artist was to tell the truth. But the RAR leadership's marxist politics also led them to the view that an honestly realistic description of the state of things would *necessarily* imply a leftist politics. Thus, for RAR all Pursey needed to do was to follow through his existing insight to its (socialist) conclusion.

This position, like Pursey's own, lacked an awareness of the creative and moulding power of ideology.[36]

Radical culture

Only eight years separate RAR from the militant counter-cultural struggles of 1968. Several of the organisation's founders were directly involved in these events, and the cocktail of mass political mobilisation

and artistic experimentation that became emblematic of that year was
an abiding influence on their lives. It is unsurprising, then, that when
the opportunity came to build a movement like RAR, it received an
enthusiastic response from these individuals. In this way some staples
of the 1960s underground, such as the use of political theatre, highly
amplified rock music and innovative visual communication, came to
characterise RAR activities. Looking back at his experiences during the
1960s, David Widgery describes an attitude that has clear affinities with
RAR's outlook:

> I had a fairly classic political conception of class struggle and that change
> of power would be extra-parliamentary. But I was also convinced that in
> the modern post-electronic cultures all our previous imagery of revolutions
> had been very Russian and that we needed to look around for new kinds
> of ways of transmitting our ideas, a new imagery and new techniques.
> I saw the underground press as a disseminator of subversive ideas.[37]

What underlay RAR's mission was, in a sense, an attempt to give new
substance to protest singer 'Country' Joe McDonald's vision of 'a cultural, political and musical fusion',[38] a social space within which popular
music could be used for progressive political ends. In enacting this
principle RAR was, to some extent, defining itself against other tendencies on the left. The British Communist Party had a history of animosity
to rock music, with many Communists viewing it as an inherently reactionary product of American cultural imperialism.[39] On the other hand
a group calling itself Music For Socialism (MFS), which adopted a
critical position towards RAR, took the view that rock could be rallied
to the cause, but adopted an explicitly elitist position towards youth
culture, with one of its theorists denouncing punk rock as fascist.[40] This
identification of punk rock with the far-right was not an isolated position on the left; the Italian Trotskyist Nemesio Ala made a similar claim
in 1977, in the magazine *Quotidiano dei Lavoratori*.[41]

Of course the 'spirit of 68' cannot be reduced to a single political
position and Jon Savage, in his history of the Sex Pistols, suggests how
one element of this political melange – the idiosyncratic anarchism of
the Situationist International – may have traversed the decades, via the
ideological sensibilities of punk's metropolitan elite.[42] If we take at face
value Malcolm McLaren et al's commitment to Situationist anarchism
we can infer that this strand of politics came to inflect the cultural
milieu in which RAR operated.[43] Widgery, however, strikes a sceptical
note regarding McLaren's radicalism, seeing in his espousal of 'sub-
situationism' a way of giving an ideological gloss to his otherwise
straightforwardly mercenary desire to 'steal musical ideas cheap and sell

them expensive'.[44] McLaren himself, a former market trader and pro-
prietor of the 'Sex' clothes shop in London's Kings Road at the time he
put the Sex Pistols together, lends weight to Widgery's estimation of his
politics. When commenting on early squabbles over the Sex Pistols'
name (Johnny Rotten wanted to drop the 'Pistols' part) McLaren
declares, 'I was in control . . . I was out to sell lots of trousers'.[45]

If the example of the 1960s underground helped to shape RAR, the
socialists who pioneered the movement were also influenced by much
older models. As Widgery has made plain, he and his fellow activists
saw in RAR an opportunity to appropriate, and to some extent reinvent,
a radical cultural heritage that could be traced back to the revolutionary
upheavals of the early twentieth century. The graphics of Rodchenko
and El Lissitsky, the poetry of Mayakovsky and the polemical imagery
of Grosz and Heartfield, all inspired RAR's attempts to create an imaginative fusion of politics and art.[46] Paul Gilroy, for one, praises RAR's
creative output and particularly its use of montage, seeing in this form
a way of reproducing 'the fragments of RAR's own contradictory constituency while conveying the discontinuity and diversity of the complex
social and political process in which a growing British authoritarianism
was being generated'.[47] But while Gilroy is clear that this represents
more than a simple plagiarisation of punk's 'cut and paste' aesthetic, he
doesn't make an explicit connection between RAR and the politically
radical modernists with whom Widgery and his comrades identified.

A concern with reviving the achievements of past generations,
and refracting them through the prism of post-1960s popular culture,
lies behind the 'three commandments' that Widgery claims were RAR's
guide:

> Vladimir Mayakovsky's admonition, 'The streets are our brushes and the
> squares our palettes,' Wilhelm Reich's advice, 'Politicise private life, fairs,
> dance-halls, cinemas, markets, bedrooms, hostels, betting shops! Revolu-
> tionary energy lies in everyday life,' and the French students' 1968 barri-
> cade cry, 'All power to the imagination!'[48]

Dave Renton has drawn attention to RAR's debt to radical modernist
antecedents, particularly those which flowered in Weimar Germany, and
implicit in his account of fascism and anti-fascism is a parallel between
the cultural coalition that RAR was assembling and those avant-garde
artists who were persecuted as degenerates by Hitler's Nazis.[49] In contrast to the stolid philistinism of the fascist right, Widgery invites us to
see RAR as an attempt to develop a joyful and emancipatory politics,
harnessing the power of ideas and rooted in the material reality of
people's lives. Widgery's emphasis on sensual pleasure and creativity

and his evocation of the spirit of the 1960s, draws a line between RAR and the 'No Fun, No Future philosophy of the NF'.[50] But he also addresses much of the left when he warns:

> If socialism is transmitted in a doleful, pre-electronic idiom, if its emotional appeal is to working-class sacrifice and middle-class guilt, and if its dominant medium is the ill-printed word and the drab public procession, it will simply bounce off people who have grown up on this side of the sixties watershed and leave barely a dent behind it.[51]

Youth culture and multiculturalism

Dick Hebdige famously described post-war British youth cultures as 'a succession of differential responses to the black immigrant presence in Britain'.[52] Whether or not we entirely accept Hebdige's formulation, we have to acknowledge that there is no analytical route to take that will allow us to consider youth culture in isolation from the multicultural matrix from which it emerges. RAR itself was founded in defence of the proposition that popular culture and multiculturalism went hand in hand. This found expression in RAR's policy of arranging gigs that jointly featured black and white acts; a practice that Widgery maintains was facilitated by the growing affinity between punk rock and reggae. The historical and social circumstances that underlay this subcultural partnership were analysed and investigated through the columns of RAR's journal, *Temporary Hoarding*. In *Beating Time* David Widgery elaborates RAR's approach to this issue and in doing so he repeats the magazine's strong emphasis on Britain's imperial heritage as a crucial factor. According to Widgery, the social maelstrom that was whipped into being by the British Empire's aggressive incursions into non-European territories created new, hybrid forms of expression, at the same time as the socio-economic processes of capitalist imperialism proletarianised millions of its new subjects, thus putting them on the same class footing as white metropolitan workers. The solidarity that RAR tried to encourage was thus, in Widgery's estimation, not simply the product of an over-riding moral imperative, or the fortuitous outcome of an essentially aesthetic doctrine, but an extension of class allegiances being formed through the consolidation of the new global economic order.

RAR did not simply debate its ideas, but tried to enact them. A RAR gig, therefore, was not envisioned as simply a concert plus political paper sellers; it represented a liberated space within which the fecundity of free cultural exchange could be demonstrated and experienced. By approaching the political through the personal in this way, RAR attempted to fly under the radar screen of knee-jerk, apolitical cynicism that disaffected youths were liable to deploy. Widgery explained RAR's approach in this way:

> What lent RAR its particular urgency was that it wasn't just fund raising for a good cause out there but we were defending and thereby redefining ourselves and the cultural mix of the inner cities in which we had grown up and in which our children are now finding their feet.[53]

And later:

> Other people and other generations are shaped by different passions, fashions and political movements. But our experience has taught us a golden political rule: how people find their pleasure, entertainment and celebration is also how they find their sexual identity, their political courage and their strength to change.[54]

Such a sentiment may have had considerable rhetorical power, but it also confirmed the suspicions of those of Widgery's critics who believed that he had overstepped the mark in making extravagant claims on behalf of popular culture. As one reviewer put it 'pop is first and last, and quite properly, youngsters having fun. Revolutionaries don't dance.'[55]

Commentators are divided over the degree to which RAR was tapping into subcultures that were fused at some fundamental level. The idea that punk and reggae, the two pre-eminent rebel youth cultures of the 1970s, had enough in common to render them natural allies in the fight against racism is a feature of several accounts. Despite their differing interpretations and emphases, this notion has been aired in Gilroy, Hebdige and, as already indicated, Widgery.

Paul Gilroy's analysis of the punk/reggae axis stresses the ways in which punks satirised and criticised the ideas and symbols of British nationalism – through their desecration of the union jack and mockery of royalty, for example. This rebellious spirit was exercised partly through a creative reworking of the 'language and style of roots culture in general and Rastafari in particular'.[56] What resulted from this endorsement of radical black culture was, in Dick Hebdige's estimation, a 'symbolic act of treason which complemented, indeed completed, the sacrilegious programme in punk rock itself'.[57] Underlying this union on the plane of aesthetics was a shared experience of social crisis within a post-imperial context. A formative flashpoint occurred in 1976, when the Notting Hill Carnival erupted in anti-police rioting and the embryonic punk movement was, according to Gilroy, given a lesson in 'the fundamental continuity of cultural expression with political action'.[58] These themes of cross-cultural fertilisation are frequently cited by cultural commentators and they are evident in David Widgery's observation that 'the post-war migration is the foreign body around which a new British identity is crystallising'.[59]

Both Hebdige and Widgery emphasise that the cultural formations taking shape amongst black and white youth existed in a state of tension. Punk didn't simply rework reggae directly, but sometimes developed, stylistically, in an antithetical manner, positing 'reggae as a "present absence"', to use Hebdige's phrase.[60] In this way the themes and attitudes of reggae became enmeshed in a musical style that was, at times, exaggeratedly 'white'. The 'cultural car crash' from which punk was emerging was not a place of repose, and what can be described by Hebdige in the language of semiotic discourse is evident in Widgery's account through the reminiscences of RAR supporters, who carried their arguments to Britain's bars and clubs and tested their resolve in physical confrontations with Nazis. In his account of the history and politics of anti-racist social movements since the 1970s, the sociologist Max Farrar pays tribute to the positive influence that white and black music fans exerted on one another:

> The explosion all over the country of RAR reggae/punk gigs, where dread-locked blacks and safety-pinned whites enthusiastically shared the same space for the first time effectively expelled both the nazi regalia and the actual Nazis from the movement.

And furthermore:

> these movements created a new form of politics: the cultural politics of everyday life. Although RAR deserves the credit for translating this into mass politics, Caribbean reggae musicians such as Bob Marley and Peter Tosh and the poet Linton Kwesi Johnson initially established the fusion of cultural activity and political commitment in the early 1970s.[61]

Some commentators, however, have questioned the extent to which punk and reggae were, in the absence of RAR's and the SWP's influence, strongly bound by common goals and interests. Frith and Street, Denselow, and particularly Sabin, all take issue with the idea that punk and reggae shared the kinds of strong cultural affinities that Gilroy and others claim to detect. In Frith and Street's estimation, for instance, RAR legitimised certain musical forms as suitable vehicles for protest, only insofar as they conformed to preconceived notions of 'authenticity'.

> For RAR, the value of a musical form lay in the proletarian authority of its performers – soul and R&B expressed the Afro-American working class; reggae expressed the Afro-Caribbean working class; punk the white working class. Music without such roots was worthless.[62]

According to Frith and Street, what these styles shared was not so much a common class basis, which set them apart from other types of popular music, but an arbitrarily assigned position within an ideological hierarchy constructed by RAR. The upshot of this prescriptive regime was that RAR concerts never featured mass-appeal, 'proletarian forms' of culture such as heavy metal and disco. Frith and Street also claim that these ideological constraints had 'an offputting effect for Asian British youth',[63] which, as we have seen, is a point strongly developed by Kalra et al and picked up by Roger Sabin.

Regarding punk's dynamism, Robin Denselow places less store in any trans-ethnic bond with Caribbean musical forms, than similarities with traditions such as folk music and skiffle, both of which, like punk rock, embodied a strong DIY ethic.[64] This reliance on the energy and enthusiasm of an exceptionally active base of supporters and artists suggests another point of contact between punk and the political philosophy of RAR's founders. Many of those flocking to RAR's banner were animated by a determination to break with the left's 'routinism', thus Red Saunders cites punk's grassroots creativity as one of the four processes that were most responsible for the movement's success.[65] For a campaign with one foot in radical politics and another in popular music, the alternative (however partial and compromised) that punk offered to the established networks of the 'culture industry', will have presented a rare challenge to capitalism's command of the channels of cultural distribution and production.

If Frith and Street emphasise RAR's failure to extend its anti-racist cultural alliance beyond a narrow compass, Sabin is concerned with the ways in which the punk wing of the movement had to be shoe-horned into its RAR-ordained role. He affirms that many punk rockers were sincere anti-racists, but claims that any inter-ethnic synergy was either purely contingent – the outcome of the musical preferences of a small punk elite – or else imaginary – a product of the mythologising process initiated mainly by politically biased journalists and commentators. What started life as an attempt by punk's chroniclers to rescue an important subculture from the clutches of widely pervasive racism was soon transformed into one of the foundation stones of RAR's cultural policy and a staple of punk mythology down to this day. Sabin charts the progress of this myth as punk became nostalgically recycled and important works of analysis and history began to appear, particularly David Widgery's *Beating Time* and Dick Hebdige's *Subculture*. He also suggests that many artists who flirted with the themes and symbols of fascism during the 1970s had strong reasons for seeing the evidence obscured or given a benign twist, not least because of the damage that such indiscretions might have caused to their commercial ambitions and their attempts to fashion consumer-friendly identities for themselves in the post-punk era (Adam Ant is an example of this latter trend).

Even where the 'punk/black culture' interface was apparently strongest, along the border with reggae, Sabin casts doubt on the popularity of Afro-Caribbean music among punks and he calls into question the ideological commitment of those who attended RAR concerts featuring punk and reggae acts, claiming that for many of them the *craic* was at least as important as the cause. We need to acknowledge, however, that the distinction Sabin has made between fun and politics represents a contradiction that RAR was determined to overcome. Widgery's remark that, 'how people find their pleasure, entertainment and celebration is also how they find their sexual identity, their political courage and their strength to change', suggests strongly that he was striving to explicate the links between individual and communal identities, and between personal and social liberation. Writing in 1978, following the first RAR/ANL carnival in April of that year, he gives vent to his frustration with socialists who abandon an active engagement in politics and culture, in favour of abstract theorising and academic respectability:

> Sometimes it has seemed, in the political dog days of the last three years, that the Marxist Left divided between those disappearing headlong into Lacan and Althusser and those reading the stoned codes of Dillinger, Peter Tosh and the Clash. It was apparent on 30th April who had made the right connection.[66]

Returning to the central plank of Sabin's argument, several critics have contradicted his claim that there exists a myth which holds 'that despite some posturing with swastikas, punk was essentially solid with the anti-racist cause'. Widgery's account, for all its occasional rhetorical flourishes, makes it plain that RAR regarded punk as a focus of conflict between left and right. 'It was another response to the same social crisis which produced the NF's successes *and it could go in any direction*'[67] was how he described the situation. Simplistic claims for punk's inherent leftism are rare in the literature, and one reviewer has even described Sabin's argument as a 'ridiculous contention'.[68] Sabin, in any case, has modified his view that commentators on British punk have been virtually unanimous in their equation of punk rock and anti-racism, conceding that he 'went too far' in making such an assertion.[69]

Punks' attitudes towards Afro-Caribbean music are controversial, but Lloyd Bradley, in his encyclopaedic history of reggae, *Bass Culture*, proposes a more positive interpretation than that offered by Sabin. Bradley claims that RAR and punk rock were associated with an explosion of interest in reggae music amongst white youth, without which, the author declares, reggae music could not have achieved the level of commercial success it did during the 1970s and 1980s. Bradley has drawn on extensive interviews with reggae artists and entrepreneurs, who found themselves faced with a large and enthusiastic audience of white fans. Reggae retailer Rae Cheddie, speaking of his experience running a record shop near London's Portobello Road, recalls:

> I loved it. I'd never taken reggae into an environment like that before, and the punk kids were so into it. They were knowledgeable, too; they'd come in and know exactly what they wanted but then they'd still be keen to hear what I could recommend. They liked their heavy dub, but they'd go for the more unusual stuff, and they were more open minded than a lot of my black customers who just wanted the new Gregory Isaacs.[70]

The artistic interplay between the different musical 'communities', which was often enacted through the medium of RAR gigs, enriched the work of all those involved and, according to Bradley, it led to some of reggae's most innovative and enduring accomplishments.[71] This flow of inspiration and influence ran in both directions, however, as reggae DJ and film maker Don Letts recalls: 'you could hear the influence of reggae on the early punk bands – in the heavy basslines, in the rebellious lyrics, and in the idea of songs as musical reportage'.[72]

Summary

A number of common themes emerge from the writings I have discussed, but also significant disagreements. It should be noted, however, that most of the critics I have discussed approach the subject of RAR from a shared commitment to, or at least sympathy with, the cause of anti-racism, and this sets limits to the scope of their criticisms. Although a handful of commentators have viewed RAR as a wholly negative influence, or a cynical political manoeuvre, most writers who have taken issue with RAR's politics, or its cultural policy, have acknowledged that RAR made a positive contribution to the pursuit of a more tolerant society.

When viewed as a popular-cultural phenomenon, it is accepted that punk rock and reggae were key components of RAR's success, but what is not agreed is the degree to which these musical and lifestyle trends contributed their own political and radical charge to the anti-racist project. For some writers, punk and reggae were seized upon by RAR's leadership and acquired a veneer of socialist consciousness as a consequence. It is a matter for debate how far RAR's politics were accepted by the artists they worked with, or to what extent this progressive partnership has been manufactured through a process of mythologisation. Doubts have also been raised over young people's commitment to the politics of a movement that offered the incentive of cheap concerts featuring popular musical acts. Some observers, though, have claimed that RAR was not so much imposing a set of values on the situation from outside, but rather exploiting the radical potential that was an internal feature of certain strands of youth culture. Even here, though, critics have argued over RAR's contribution; some seeing it as a catalyst for further positive developments, and others believing that it inhibited or diverted the spontaneous radicalism of the young.

As we have seen, there are sharp disagreements over the extent to which RAR succeeded in its aim of forging a broad and inclusive cultural united front. The absence from RAR concert platforms of musical forms such as disco, not to mention Asian music, has been adduced by some as evidence that the organisation was at best elitist and at worst, implicitly racist. For someone like David Widgery, however, the effortless multiculturalism of the post-RAR music scene is a testament to the movement's positive influence.

Relatively little has been said about the content of RAR's politics, perhaps because so much of the discussion has come from a cultural studies perspective. The close personal and political ties between RAR and the SWP have been noted in various places, and although disagreements remain over the extent of RAR's autonomy, researchers at the UEA and testimony from RAR supporters and others suggests that RAR was able to exploit political and cultural networks that existed independently of the organisation. It is noticeable that there have been few attempts to define the precise affinities between RAR and other left-wing experiments in cultural politics, or to discuss those aspects of the SWP's politics that may have influenced its work on the cultural front. This gap in the literature makes it difficult to properly assess the ways in which political and cultural theory have combined with particular forms of practical activity in giving rise to the RAR phenomenon. Widgery's assertion that 'RAR cured the schizophrenia between Marxist politics and modern culture'[73] is apt to seem not only rather exaggerated, but it also raises the question of why there should have been such a strained relationship between popular culture and politics in the first place.

Notes

1 Cited in Renton, *When We Touched the Sky*, p. 50.
2 See Gilroy, *There Ain't No Black*, ch 4.
3 Nigel Copsey, *Anti-Fascism in Britain* (Macmillan, Basingstoke, 2000), p. 135.

4 Dave Renton, *When We Touched the Sky*, pp. 126–128.

5 David Widgery, Ruth Gregory, Syd Shelton and Roger Huddle, 'Look get it straight', *Socialist Review* (July/August 1978), p. 14.

6 Ian Birchall, 'Only rock 'n' roll? A review of D. Widgery, Beating Time', in *International Socialism Journal*, 2:33 (Autumn 1986), p. 127.

7 Birchall, 'Only Rock', p. 131.

8 Pat Stack, 'Rocking the racists', *Socialist Review* (July/August 1986), p. 30.

9 Ashley Dawson, ' "Love Music, Hate Racism": The cultural politics of the Rock Against Racism campaigns, 1976–1981', *Postmodern Culture*, 16:1 (September 2005), www3.iath.virginia.edu/pmc/current.issue/16.1dawson. html, downloaded 26 May 2006.

10 Hanif Kureishi, 'Without deference', *Times Literary Supplement* (8 August 1986; Chatto & Windus reviews: 1986); Ken Leech, 'Beat time', *Crucible* (January–March 1987; Chatto & Windus reviews: 1986); Virinder S. Kalra, John Hutnyk and Sanjay Sharma, 'Re-sounding (anti) racism, or concordant politics?', in S. Sharma, J. Hutnyk and A. Sharma (eds), *Dis-orienting Rhythms: The politics of the new Asian dance music* (Zed Books, London, 1996).

11 Stewart Home, *We Mean It Man: Punk rock and anti-racism – or Death In June not mysterious*, www.stewarthomesociety.org/man.htm, downloaded 3 August 2007.

12 Fred Lindop, 'Racism and the working class: strikes in support of Enoch Powell', *Labour History Review*, 66:1 (2001); Evan Smith, 'Fighting oppression wherever it exists: The Communist Party of Great Britain and the struggle against racism, 1962–1981', *Eras Online Journal*, 7 (November 2005), available as a download: www.arts.monash.edu.au/eras/edition_7/ smitharticle.htm, downloaded 27 May 2006.

13 The following discussion draws on Copsey, *Anti-Fascism*, pp. 123–126 and Renton, *When We Touched the Sky*, pp. 23–31.

14 Ian Birchall, *Building 'The Smallest Mass Party in the World': Socialist Workers Party 1951–1979*. This pamphlet, published in 1981, is available online at www.revolutionary-history.co.uk/otherdox/SMP/Smp1.html, downloaded 2 March 2008.

15 For an account of the strike and its aftermath, see Jack Dromey and Graham Taylor, *Grunwick: The workers' story* (Lawrence and Wishart, London, 1978).

16 Dave Renton, *When We Touched the Sky*, pp. 29–30.

17 The following discussion draws on John Street, Seth Hague, Heather Savigny, 'Playing to the crowd: the role of music and musicians in political participation', *The British Journal of Politics and International Relations*, 10:2 (May 2008).

18 Street, Hague, Savigny, 'Playing to the Crowd', p. 278.

19 Ibid.

20 Ibid., p. 279.

21 *Temporary Hoarding*, No. 6 (Summer 1978). See also: www.planetgong. co.uk/octave/gighistory/1978.shtml#august, downloaded 9 November 2007.

22 Street, Hague, Savigny, 'Playing to the Crowd', p. 279.
23 *Sounds* (25 March 1978).
24 Gareth Dent, personal communication (31 October 2007).
25 Frith and Street, 'Rock Against Racism and Red Wedge', p. 67.
26 Ibid., p. 70.
27 Denselow, *When the Music's Over*, p. 144.
28 Ibid., p. 140.
29 Sabin, *Punk Rock: So What?*, pp. 203–206.
30 Ibid., p. 205.
31 See for example: Ali Rattansi, 'Changing the subject? Racism, culture and education', in Donald and Rattansi, *'Race', Culture and Difference*; and C.W. Watson, *Multiculturalism* (Open University Press, Buckingham, 2000), ch 2.
32 Kalra et al, *Dis-orienting Rhythms*, p. 153.
33 Sabin, *Punk Rock: So What?*, p. 207.
34 Savage, *England's Dreaming*, p. 483.
35 Ibid., p. 481.
36 Dave Laing, *One Chord Wonders: Power and meaning in punk rock* (Open University Press, Milton Keynes, 1985), p. 111.
37 Jonathon Green, *Days in the Life: Voices from the English underground 1961–1971* (Heinemann, London, 1988), p. 256.
38 This is McDonald's description of radical 1960s San Francisco, in Denselow, *When the Music's Over*, p. 68.
39 For contrasting assessments of the British Communist Party's role in sponsoring the post-war folk-song revival as a counter-balance to the prevalence of American popular culture, see: Gerald Porter, 'The world's ill-divided: The Communist Party and progressive song', in Andy Croft (ed.), *A Weapon in the Struggle: The cultural history of the Communist Party in Britain* (Pluto Press, London, 1998), ch 10; Dave Harker, *One For the Money: Politics and popular song* (Hutchinson, London, 1980), ch 9; Michael Brocken, *The British Folk Revival: 1944–2002* (Ashgate, Aldershot, 2003).
40 Frith and Street, 'Rock Against Racism and Red Wedge', p. 68.
41 Dave Renton, *When We Touched the Sky*, p. 44.
42 Savage, *England's Dreaming*, passim.
43 Stewart Home is entirely sceptical about the supposed link between Situationism and punk rock, and he devotes a chapter of his book on punk to explaining why. See: Home, *Cranked Up Really High*, ch 2.
44 Widgery, *Beating Time*, p. 64.
45 Savage, *England's Dreaming*, p. 129.
46 Widgery, *Beating Time*, ch 4.
47 Paul Gilroy, *There Ain't No Black in the Union Jack: The cultural politics of race and nation* (Routledge, London, 1992), p. 128.
48 Widgery, *Beating Time*, p. 53.
49 Dave Renton, *This Rough Game: Fascism and Anti-Fascism* (Sutton Publishing, Stroud, 2001), chs 8 and 13.

50 Widgery, *Beating Time*, p. 86.
51 Ibid., p. 84.
52 Dick Hebdige, *Subculture: The meaning of style* (Methuen, London, 1979), p. 29.
53 Widgery, *Beating Time*, pp. 55–56.
54 Ibid., p. 56.
55 Brian Morton, 'Agents of change', *Times Educational Supplement* (11 July 1986; Chatto & Windus reviews: 1986). See also Ian Bell, 'Rocking against the right', *The Scotsman* (17 June 1986; Chatto & Windus reviews: 1986); Ian Birchall, 'Only rock 'n' roll?'; Pat Stack, 'Rocking the racists'; Michael Poole, 'Keeping the Beat', *The Listener* (5 June 1986; Chatto & Windus reviews: 1986).
56 Gilroy, *There Ain't No Black*, p. 123.
57 Hebdige, *Subculture*, p. 64.
58 Gilroy, *There Ain't No Black*, p. 125.
59 Widgery, *Beating Time*, p. 119.
60 Hebdige, *Subculture*, p. 68.
61 Max Farrar, *Social Movements and the Struggle Over 'Race'*, www.maxfarrar.org.uk/mywork_academicarticles.htm, downloaded 24 July 2007.
62 Frith and Street, 'Rock Against Racism and Red Wedge', p. 76.
63 Ibid., p. 69.
64 Denselow, *When the Music's Over*, p. 148.
65 Renton, *When We Touched the Sky*, p. 35. The other three processes given by Saunders are: the political experience of radicals who had been active in the 1960s, the 'unequivocal support' of the SWP, and the RAR/ANL carnivals.
66 David Widgery, 'Letter From Britain: Carnival against the Nazis', *Radical America*, 12:5 (September–October 1978), p. 77.
67 Widgery, *Beating Time*, p. 61 (my emphasis).
68 Stewart Home, *Review of Roger Sabin, editor, Punk Rock: So What?*, http://stewarthomesociety.org/punk1.htm, downloaded 3 August 2007.
69 Sabin, personal communication (29 June 2001).
70 Bradley, *Bass Culture*, p. 450.
71 Ibid., ch 18.
72 'Voices from Rock Against Racism', www.socialistworker.co.uk/art.php?id=12353, downloaded 14 July 2007.
73 Widgery, *Beating Time*, p. 56.

3

Rock Against Racism and the Socialist Workers Party

Although RAR's relationship with the SWP has been the subject of much comment, the political and organisational aspects of this connection have, to date, received relatively little attention. Since the party played an important part in RAR and the wider anti-racist movement during the 1970s, this absence of an analytical overview hinders our understanding of both organisations and it restricts our understanding of the British left in general. It may seem peculiar, after all, that the most spectacular and successful anti-racist movements of the 1970s – RAR and the ANL – should have been initiated by a small and dissident group of Trotskyists, with only a fraction of the political and logistical resources of more influential sections of the workers' movement such as the Communist Party and the left wing of the Labour Party.

It is worth emphasising at this point that my argument is *not* that RAR was a mere party front – as will become clear throughout this book – but instead to suggest why many SWP members were able to operate effectively along sections of the politico-cultural spectrum that were generally off-limits to large parts of the left. It may be that one of the reasons behind this is the relative lack of that conservative inertia which, to a greater or lesser extent, afflicts large organisations. While this may be the case, I will argue that the SWP's role in RAR had more to do with the party's political ideas and the socio-economic context of the mid-1970s than any merely contingent factor such as the size of the organisation.

One of the gaps in previous surveys of RAR and the part played in the movement by the SWP is their failure to offer a convincing account of the movement's politics. To be fair, this isn't a goal that authors have generally set for themselves, although the kinds of simplistic caricatures of the left in general, and of Marxism in particular, that sometimes occur in histories of the music scene need to be challenged (Simon Reynolds's glib reference to 'right on trendy leftism' is a case in point).[1] If we are to grasp the nature of the RAR/SWP link we need to go beyond simplifying assumptions – for instance, that there is a single body of

Marxist political and aesthetic theory, from which RAR's founders drew – and appreciate instead what was distinctive in the SWP's mix of theory and practice and relate this to the social and political context of the late 1970s. By so doing we can see how a shift in the party's emphasis, from industrial to political struggles, came about and how this led to a more rigorous engagement with issues of oppression, such as racism. It is at this point that party members helped to launch anti-racist initiatives such as RAR and the ANL.

This chapter is divided into two sections. The first deals with important theoretical issues that are particularly pertinent to the party's relationship with RAR; these cover three areas: the theory of state capitalism, the relationship between the party and the working class, and the united front. The second section examines the state of the Socialist Workers Party – formerly the International Socialists (IS)[2] – during the mid- to late 1970s. I suggest how the SWP attempted to relate its theory to events in the world at large and how these events, in turn, shaped the party's interventions. I have dealt with those elements of the SWP's politics that I believe are most relevant to our understanding of the party's relationship with RAR and I have attempted to highlight those areas that distinguished the SWP from other sections of the left in Britain. In what follows I am not suggesting that there is a straightforwardly causal link between theory and practice, but rather that the SWP's politics had a significant effect upon its attitude towards mass movements such as RAR. Nor do I wish to imply that RAR's politics were synonymous with the SWP's, for this is patently not the case – the breadth of opinion organised under the RAR umbrella alone undermines such a view. I do feel, however, that the unevenness of the British left's response to racism demands an explanation, and that the SWP's ability to respond effectively to the rise of the NF in the 1970s deserves close scrutiny.

State capitalism and the relationship between party and class

Apparently arcane disputes among socialists over the nature of post-revolutionary Russia's social system may seem an odd diversion during a discussion about anti-racism in 1970s Britain. I would suggest, however, that the ways in which socialists in the aftermath of World War Two characterised the Russian state and consequently interpreted the dynamics of international politics are relevant to our investigation. It is the case after all, that the ambivalence of much of the left towards certain forms of mass culture – such as crime comics, Hollywood movies, and rock music – stemmed in large part from the perception that they were products of US cultural imperialism and as such were implicated in America's struggle against Russian Communism and progressive movements generally.[3] Although Stalinists and orthodox Trotskyists felt a bitter enmity towards one another over most things, both camps, in their different ways, shared an underlying belief that the Soviet Union represented a qualitative advance beyond capitalism. Whereas Communists and their fellow-travellers viewed Russia as a bastion of socialism,[4] Trotskyists saw it as a transitional form, a 'degenerated workers' state', rather than fully socialist.[5] Although these positions were opposed in certain ways, they both carried the implication that socialists in the west owed Russia their unconditional (if sometimes critical) support. For Communists in particular, this duty extended to a struggle against American cultural hegemony, which inevitably entailed not only a rejection of the products of the United States' culture industries, but also the validation and promulgation of aesthetic doctrines and cultural forms deemed acceptable by Moscow.

If the pro-Soviet politics of much of the left had consequences for international questions, they also had an obvious and direct influence on socialists' view of the role played by workers in effecting social change. Communists and Trotskyists alike claimed that the preponderance of nationalised property in Russia was the key determinant in defining the nation's social character. Inevitably this implied a shift in focus, away from the working class and towards the state and other bureaucratic structures. So, when a Stalinist economic and social model was imposed throughout eastern Europe following the Second World War it became difficult, even for Stalinism's Trotskyist critics, to avoid the conclusion that a new tranche of 'deformed workers' states' had been established, but without the active, revolutionary involvement of the working class. As the Polish writer Czeslaw Milosz put it: 'This was, indeed, a peculiar Revolution . . . it was carried out entirely by official decree'.[6] It seemed, therefore, that Red Army tanks and political intrigue were more effective agents of revolution than the proletariat.[7]

In 1948, and in opposition to both Communism and the orthodox Trotskyism of the Fourth International, Tony Cliff, one of the IS's founders, proposed that Russia was a highly centralised state capitalist economy governed by a bureaucratic class, which performed its exploitative role collectively. Although Cliff accepted the proletarian credentials of the October Revolution, he believed that the regime's international isolation had strangled it and prepared the ground for Stalinist counter-revolution. The measures undertaken by the rising Stalinist bureaucracy to secure the regime's survival in the face of international competition were, according to Cliff, the (highly accelerated) equivalent of the process of 'primitive accumulation' of capital that had occurred in Britain in the centuries before capitalism became fully consolidated there.[8] Thus, measures like the complete eradication of workers' control over industry, the forced collectivisation of Russian agriculture and, from 1928 onwards, a series of five-year plans that subordinated workers' interests to the demands of their rulers, broke the link between the 1917 revolution and the brutal system that was built on its ruins. Viewed in isolation, conditions within Russia resembled those within a single huge enterprise, thus presenting a social model without the competition between multiple enterprises typically associated with capitalism. However, on an international scale the Soviet Union was one part of a global economy, and despite its striving for economic autarchy it could not escape the necessity of maintaining its position relative to other countries, particularly the USA. Given intense imperialist rivalry, one of the sharpest expressions of economic competition was a massively costly arms race between east and west. It was powerful influences such as these that obliged the Russian state to behave as any other bourgeois concern. Having established an essential symmetry between Stalinism and its more overtly capitalist competitors, Cliff and his co-thinkers concluded that the Russian proletariat was, therefore, functionally identical to working classes elsewhere and it needed to overthrow the Russian ruling class using similar revolutionary methods.[9]

The theory of state capitalism certainly led Cliff and the IS to reject any urge to automatically privilege the cultures of Stalinist societies, but the flip-side of their rejection of one left-wing shibboleth was that they were also insulated from much of the left's unreflective anti-Americanism. This attempt to chart an independent course through the treacherous waters of cold-war politics is summed up in the IS slogan: 'Neither Washington nor Moscow but international socialism'. Such a stance did not close the door to formulating a class-conscious position on cultural matters, but it did mean that 'Americanised' forms of art and entertainment were not condemned *a priori* as less 'valid' than other countries'. When it came to relating to young workers in Britain, the IS tendency, therefore, carried less, potentially cumbersome, political and 'cultural baggage' than the CP.[10]

In rejecting the left's fetishism of the state the IS attempted to revivify the 'classical' Marxist tradition, which held that 'the emancipation of the working class must be the act of the workers themselves'.[11] Accordingly, Cliff and his comrades developed an orientation on grassroots activism within the workers' movement and society at large. The result was, according to a leading member of the party today, a political tendency in which 'the implied commitment to the construction of a revolutionary party was combined with a Luxemburgian stress on the essential and creative role played by spontaneous explosions of working-class revolt'.[12] How the IS's strategic perspective was to be enacted could

vary according to circumstances, but its goal of developing a political
leadership within the massed ranks of the labour movement meant
the revolutionary party had to be conceived of as an organisation of
activists, rather than abstract theoreticians or sectarians.

Bourgeois ideology and revolutionary organisation

One of the problems faced by the left is that it deals in ideas that run
counter to the 'common-sense' notions which routinely prevail under
capitalism. The hierarchies of power that dominate our relationships at
work, at home and in our dealings with the state seem not merely ubiq-
uitous, but also 'natural'. Every futile war, avoidable environmental
catastrophe, or economic crisis seems to confirm that the vast majority
of people are not in control of their destinies; that they are objects, rather
than subjects, of history. The Marxist critique of capitalism declares that
this situation is neither natural nor inevitable and it points to the role
played by bourgeois ideology in providing it a spurious legitimacy. But
if the maintenance of capitalism is so contrary to the interests of most
people, why do we not realise this? Why do we accept so readily the
ideas of a class – the bourgeoisie – which advances its own interests so
aggressively and whose rule is based upon the economic exploitation of
the majority? The solution to this mystery cannot be found solely in the
virtual monopoly enjoyed by the ruling class in its control over important cultural institutions such as schools and the mass media, although
such overbearing influence is bound to have a profound effect on the
ideas that prevail in society. More importantly, according to Marx, the
central definitive act of capitalism, generalised commodity production,
is also, and simultaneously, a process through which the proletariat sur-
renders control over its life to the class enemy.

Commodity production, which is to say production for an impersonal
market rather than to meet the needs of the direct producers, should
not be conceived as a straightforwardly economic process; it has social,
ideological and political ramifications, too. Marx insists that what sepa-
rates us from all other animals is our ability to engage in conscious
labour, to shape the world around us according to more-or-less clearly
articulated plans and desires.

> An animal forms objects only in accordance with the standard and the
> need of the species to which it belongs, whilst man knows how to produce
> in accordance with the standard of every species, and knows how to apply
> everywhere the inherent standard to the object. Man therefore also forms
> objects in accordance with the laws of beauty.[13]

Capitalism, however, estranges workers from the means of production. It places control over society's productive resources and over the products of labour in the hands of the bourgeoisie; and the workers, in their turn, are paid a wage in return for the labour they devote to making things for sale in the market. By estranging the proletariat from the means of production and from the products of its own labour, capitalism severs the crucial link between the individual and his or her creative capacities. Capitalism therefore denies workers their essential humanity, or as Marx puts it, their 'species-being'. It is this act of physical alienation that provides the material substrate for bourgeois ideology, where it is manifested in the realm of ideas. Marx, in his *Economic and Philosophical Manuscripts*, captures the historic sundering of humanity from its essential nature, and the way in which the products of human ingenuity and industry are turned against their creators.

> What, then, constitutes the alienation of labour?
>
> First, the fact that labour is *external* to the worker, i.e., it does not belong to his intrinsic nature; that in his work, therefore, he does not affirm himself but denies himself, does not feel content but unhappy, does not develop freely his physical and mental energy but mortifies his body and ruins his mind. The worker therefore only feels himself outside his work, and in his work feels outside himself. He feels at home when he is not working, and when he is working he does not feel at home. His labour is therefore not voluntary but coerced; it is *forced labour*. It is therefore not the satisfaction of a need; it is merely a *means* to satisfy needs external to it. Its alien character emerges clearly in the fact that as soon as no physical or other compulsion exists, labour is shunned like the plague. External labour, labour in which man alienates himself, is a labour of self-sacrifice, of mortification. Lastly, the external character of labour for the worker appears in the fact that it is not his own, but someone else's, that it does not belong to him, that in it he belongs, not to himself, but to another. Just as in religion the spontaneous activity of the human imagination, of the human brain and the human heart, operates on the individual independently of him – that is, operates as an alien, divine or diabolical activity – so is the worker's activity not his spontaneous activity. It belongs to another; it is the loss of his self.[14]

But if bourgeois ideology is deeply rooted in the material reality of capitalism, other, oppositional, forces and ideas emerge from the same circumstances. Human beings do not simply acquiesce in their own subjugation. Relentless accumulation of capital entails an equally relentless accumulation of contradictions: between wealth and poverty, freedom and wage slavery, luxury and squalor, the list is endless. These antagonisms find expression in countless acts of resistance, from petty sabotage in the workplace to full-blown revolution. It is not surprising, therefore, that people's consciousnesses share this contradictory nature. Although the ideas of the ruling class have a powerful hold on the minds of everyone under capitalism, they do not enjoy a perfect monopoly. Individual workers will, in varying degrees, hold ideas which both reinforce and undermine their subjection to capital. The Italian revolutionary Antonio Gramsci recognised the importance of this when he wrote:

> The active man-in-the-mass has a practical activity, but has no clear theoretical consciousness of his practical activity, which nonetheless involves understanding the world in so far as it transforms it. His theoretical consciousness can indeed be historically in opposition to his activity. One might almost say that he has two theoretical consciousnesses (or one contradictory consciousness): one which is implicit in his activity and which in reality unites him with all his fellow-workers in the practical transformation of the real world; and one, superficially explicit or verbal, which he has inherited from the past and uncritically absorbed. But this verbal conception is not without consequences. It holds together a specific social group, it influences moral conduct and the direction of will, with varying efficacy but often powerfully enough to produce a situation in which the contradictory state of consciousness does not permit of any action, any decision or any choice, and produces a condition of moral and political passivity.[15]

But if we accept that the vast majority of people will have a contradictory consciousness and that only a relatively small minority will be willing to break completely with bourgeois ideology in the direction of revolutionary socialism, the question for socialists is, in Lenin's phrase, what is to be done? How can small parties and tendencies, operating on the fringes of political and social acceptability, build a relationship with far less politically radical (or even engaged) masses? What organisational forms, and strategic and tactical perspectives, are best suited to maximising the influence of the revolutionary minority?

The Leninist response to the issue of party organisation (and this is the tradition to which the SWP claims allegiance) is to bring together the most class-conscious and militant members of the working class and constitute them as a revolutionary vanguard. But this is only half an answer, for even if Bolshevism provides a basic model for building a core group of revolutionaries it runs the risk of creating an inward-looking and isolated sect, with little contact with the vast, uncommitted majority of workers. Consequently, ways have to be sought to bridge the gap between party and class and the united front is one response to this challenge. We need to be careful at this point not to confuse a legitimate concern with organisational issues with a tendency to fetish-ise specific and rigidly codified means of ordering the affairs of the revolutionary party (although such a tendency is often all too evident on the left). It is not the case that Leninism, for instance, necessarily implies the endorsement of a tightly specified version of the ideal party, torn from the social and political context in which it needs to operate. Tony Cliff is eager to stress this when he writes:

> Another of Lenin's characteristics already apparent at this early stage of his development is an attitude to organizational forms as always historically determined. He never adopted abstract, dogmatic schemes of organization, and was ready to change the organizational structure of the party at every new development of the class struggle. Organization, he was convinced, should be subordinated to politics.[16]

Before going on to discuss the nature and purpose of the united front it is therefore worth emphasising that the relationship between RAR and the SWP is not a carbon copy of some long-past organisational model, but it does need to be set within a political context that was shaped by earlier debates on the left. However much RAR can be characterised as a novel form of political organisation and activism we need to be aware that the campaign was informed by the motives and intentions of socialists schooled in a particular revolutionary tradition. With this in mind we can interpret RAR as one element within a much wider-ranging attempt to shift the ideological balance within the British left and British society.

The united front

The IS tendency developed out of a split in the FI, and although this was the occasion for a great deal of acrimony it is nevertheless true that the fledgling organisation owed a great deal to the politics of both the FI and the early years of the Comintern. A part of this heritage that strongly influenced the SWP's activities during the 1970s is the theory of the united front. Formulated by the Comintern following the Russian Revolution, the united front was conceived as a method for building alliances between, primarily, revolutionary and social-democratic sections of the workers' movement, but without sacrificing the political or organisational independence of the bodies involved. The most important objective, of course, was to secure the explicitly stated goals of the alliance, but in the process revolutionaries also hoped to win sections of the working class to revolutionary ideas and to locate themselves more firmly in the day-to-day struggles of the proletariat as a whole.

For a united front to be effective requires that it defines for itself a narrow set of aims, since this allows it to appeal to people of very different political persuasions, who nevertheless recognise certain basic, common interests. What the theory of the united front assumes is that the consciousness of workers is uneven: individuals may see eye-to-eye with revolutionary socialists on a particular issue, but not on others. Hence a steadfast anti-racist may be willing to fight alongside revolutionaries in defence of immigrant workers, but reject a left-wing position on, say, women's rights. It may be tempting in these circumstances for socialists to maintain their ideological purity by isolating themselves from the contagion of less radical layers of the population; this would, however, be a mistake. At best it means failing to challenge, in the public sphere, the ideas of the existing leadership of the workers' movement; at worst it risks offering no effective resistance if workers become disillusioned with reformism and start searching for other, possibly fascist, routes out of crisis. According to supporters of the united front it is self-defeating to stand aloof from the concerns of the great majority of workers who, in most periods, will not share either the political convictions or organisational discipline of committed revolutionaries. Rather, by demonstrating in practice the superiority of revolutionary politics, socialists can hope both to win converts to socialism and to expose the weakness of other political tendencies. Writing in 1922, Trotsky explained the importance of the united front in these terms:

> If the Communist Party did not seek for organizational avenues to the end that at every given moment joint, coordinated action between the Communist and the non-Communist (including the Social-Democratic) working masses were made possible, it would have thereby laid bare its own capacity to win over – on the basis of mass action – the majority of the working class. It would degenerate into a Communist propaganda society but never develop into a party for the conquest of power.
>
> It is not enough to possess the sword, one must give it an edge; it is not enough to give the sword an edge, one must know how to wield it.
>
> After separating the Communists from the reformists it is not enough to fuse the Communists together by means of organizational discipline; it is necessary that this organization should learn how to guide all the collective activities of the proletariat in all spheres of its living struggle.[17]

Trotsky makes clear in the following passage how the united front can act as a medium for exposing the vacillation of reformist leaders:

> [W]e are, apart from all other considerations, interested in dragging the reformists from their asylums and placing them alongside ourselves before the eyes of the struggling masses. With a correct tactic we stand only to

gain from this. A Communist who doubts or fears this resembles a swimmer who has approved the theses on the best method of swimming but dares not plunge in the water.[18]

The united front, then, is necessarily aimed at securing a specific and limited end. The goal is defined in such a way as to ensure that a broad section of opinion can agree upon it, and the front is constituted on the basis that all groups retain their freedom to criticise, issue propaganda, raise slogans and so on. The aspiration is for unity in action, but without sacrificing the political independence of the various parties involved.[19]

The theory of the united front has become inextricably linked with the name of the Russian revolutionary leader Leon Trotsky, who fought desperately during his time in exile from Russia to persuade the workers' movements of Spain and Germany in particular to apply it in their struggles against fascism. In an unequal contest between competing political forces Trotsky was pitted against the vast majority of the left, including big and well-entrenched Social-Democratic parties and the Stalinist Comintern. The failures of Communist leadership in this period were both tragic and deplorable. Obedient to Stalin's orders, the global Communist movement veered from an ultra-sectarian rejection of alliances with Social-Democrats, to the pursuit of cross-class pacts with sections of the ruling class, or 'popular fronts' as they became known.[20] Rather than maintain their political and organisational independence, Communists were urged to lend support to 'progressive' elements of the bourgeoisie, whilst abandoning any of their own revolutionary aspirations. The fruits of this policy were most evident in Spain, where the Communist Party fiercely criticised and suppressed other forces on the left, even to the point of crushing them militarily. Simultaneously, the Spanish Communist Party worked hard to avoid any breach with its bourgeois allies.[21]

It would be wrong to suggest that the situation in Britain in the 1970s was anywhere near as grave as in Spain or Germany in the 1930s, but the lessons learned during that period have informed the Trotskyist left ever since. The forces of revolutionary socialism have had to come to terms with the fact that, in the post-war period, they have never attained anything like the stature they enjoyed during Trotsky's lifetime, and so they have not been able to apply pressure to reformist parties in the way envisaged in a classical united front. It is still the case, however, that Trotsky's admonitions against sectarian isolation have prompted some on the far-left to acknowledge at least the spirit, if not the precise letter, of united front theory. The people who founded RAR were by no means unanimous in their political convictions, but it would be fair to say that they were all impatient with the kinds of armchair politics practised by many on the left, particularly those who sought refuge in socialism's 'sacred texts' rather than in the messy reality of class struggle. If those RAR activists who traced their political lineage back to Trotsky and the early years of the Third International were to retain their relevance, they would be obliged to reinterpret for modern conditions, political ideas forged in the heat of earlier struggles.

The SWP and the rank and file movement

By the early 1970s all the parties to the political consensus, including the established hierarchies of the labour movement, found themselves under challenge from a self-confident rank and file within the organisations of the working class.[22] These grassroots militants, often shop stewards, had exerted a steadily growing influence within British industry since the 1950s. One consequence of this shift in the balance of power away from the centralised structures of trade unions and towards the shop floor was a tendency to bypass the 'official' machinery of industrial relations in favour of unofficial action (not authorised beforehand by the strikers' union) as a means of resolving workers' grievances.[23] The strike wave of 1968–74 saw not only a massive leap in the scale and extent of industrial action in Britain – strike days reached a peak of nearly 24 million in 1972, up from fewer than three million in 1967[24] – but it also provided conditions in which rank and file activists could consider constituting themselves as an alternative to what many saw as conservative and bureaucratic union leaderships.[25] So concerned had both the Labour and Conservative parties become about these developments, that governments of both stripes attempted to legislate against particular forms of industrial action. Labour's attempt came to grief in 1969, when its white paper *In Place of Strife* failed to gain enough support, either in parliament or the wider workers' movement, to reach the statute books.[26] In 1971 Edward Heath's Tory administration tried to suppress the growing threat to the profits and prerogatives of British capitalism, by passing an Industrial Relations Act that set out to curb the ability of workers and their unions to initiate strikes or to offer solidarity to workers already in dispute with their employers.[27] This overt intrusion of the state into industrial relations inevitably politicised the conflict between employers and employees and it led increasing numbers of workers to recognise the political implications of their ostensibly economic demands. The radicalisation of key sections of the working class in the 1970s therefore extended beyond the bread and butter issues typically associated with trade unionism, and directly political strikes became a salient feature of this new situation.[28]

In line with its theoretical perspectives, the SWP oriented itself upon the militant minority within the working class and set about building a presence among them. This was not a complete bolt from the blue, however, since a small number of SWP members in industry had been patiently carrying out such work throughout the 1960s.[29] An important step in the direction of the rank and file came in 1969, when the SWP executed a so-called 'turn to the class', through which it hoped to inculcate within its largely middle-class, student membership, a routine of activity among workers. It followed this up with recruitment drives over the next few years that succeeded in boosting membership from 880 in 1970, to 2,351 in Easter 1972.[30] Sales of the weekly *Socialist Worker* boomed in the same period, with the average print order during 1971–72 increasing from 13,000 to 28,000, which translated into an estimated readership of over 50,000.[31]

The SWP could certainly claim to have made genuine gains in the early 1970s, both in terms of working-class membership and influence upon the course of industrial struggle. In 1972 its members played a significant part in a number of disputes and campaigns, including the closure of Saltley Coke Depot. This was a pivotal moment in the history of the British labour movement, which saw key groups of workers, in solidarity with striking miners, march on the depot, thereby forcing the police to abandon attempts to keep it open and maintain fuel supplies.[32] But if the forces of the state, in the shape of the police, were being confronted on demonstrations and picket lines, they were no less evident in important legal battles, in which the SWP supported working-class militants who fell foul of both criminal and industrial laws. One such case was that of the 'Pentonville Five', a group of dockers sentenced to prison by the National Industrial Relations Court for illegally picketing a storage company.[33] For its part in a campaign resulting in the dockers' release, the SWP was accorded considerable kudos and the organisation recruited a number of key workers as a result.[34] SWP members were also prominent in the campaign to release the 'Shrewsbury Three' – building workers who were imprisoned under anti-conspiracy legislation dating back to the nineteenth century. Other instances, mostly modest, can be cited, but by 1973 the SWP felt that the wave of class conflict sweeping Britain was strong and enduring enough to warrant a shift towards factory, rather than geographical, branches of the organisation. In accordance with this optimistic assessment, the SWP organised two conferences in 1974 at which a National Rank and File

Movement (NRFM) was inaugurated. The proliferation of rank and file newspapers among significant groups of workers and an impressive roster of delegates to the conferences buttressed this expansive outlook.[35] The SWP appeared to be building an organisation that could act, in the words of one activist, as 'an excellent training ground for a national working class leadership'.[36]

The collapse of the rank and file and
the search for alternatives

Unfortunately for the SWP, its orientation on the militant rank and file within the unions reached its apogee at precisely the moment when such a perspective became fatally undermined. In truth, the rank and file movement had always represented a relatively small minority of workers, and by the time a Labour government was returned in 1974 it had failed to achieve the critical mass that would have allowed it to act completely independently of the official trade union machinery. Labour's determination to undermine the combativeness of the trade unions had not diminished since 1969, but the new government relied upon stealth rather than legislation to achieve its ends. Trade union leaders were thus invited to participate more closely in the management of the economy, and much of the machinery of the labour movement was turned away from confrontations with employers and the state and towards policing productivity deals and wage restraint.[37] Labour's rhetoric of 'participation' and its decision to bring on board important union leaders, proved far more successful than the Tories' confrontational approach in persuading workers to accept reductions in real pay, alongside public spending cuts. To understand the dynamics of this process, we need to appreciate how tenacious reformism is in such circumstances.

Reformism is the name given to the idea that capitalism can be transformed gradually, through piecemeal reforms enacted via existing organs of government such as parliament and local councils, and working alongside the institutions of the capitalist state (police, judiciary etc). Not only does reformism conform to the essential logic of bourgeois ideology, insofar as it accepts the necessity for maintaining the capitalist system; it also has an organisational embodiment in the shape of the 'official' labour movement. But within the movement there is a clear split between political and economic struggles, which in Britain is reflected in the distinction between trade unions and the Labour Party, and the leaderships of both wings of the movement strive to maintain this division of labour. In this way, workplace demands resist generalisation into broader political struggles, and the business of government is reserved for a small group of representatives kept at arm's length from the daily concerns of their working-class constituents. This distinction between politics and economics runs counter to the Marxist contention that the ruling class's *political* power is grounded in its *economic* strength, that is to say its control over the means of production. For revolutionaries to break large numbers of workers from their attachment to the 'traditional' institutions and ideas of the workers' movement requires not only that these workers confront capitalism in the workplace, but that they also draw the necessary political conclusions from this conflict. The political opposition that workers offer to capitalism should not, therefore, mimic the Labour Party in standing on a completely separate plane from the industrial wing of the movement. However, despite the left's numerous successes over the previous four years, by 1974 no convincing political alternative to Labour had emerged. Rather, most class-conscious workers still looked to left-wingers in the Labour Party, or in some cases to the Communist Party, to articulate their political demands. But since both Communists and the Labour left were keen to promote the idea of workers' participation in managing capitalism, neither could provide the kind of leadership that would have undermined the government's plans to pass on the cost of economic crisis to the working class. The staged introduction of pay restraint and stringent limits on public-sector spending did provoke resistance, but by the time this posed a serious threat to the government the organs of popular resistance were no longer strong enough to offer serious leadership. The enfeeblement of the rank and file movement can be gauged by considering the almost complete failure of the CP-led Liaison Committee for the Defence of Trade Unions' call for a national stoppage in protest at the social contract, in April 1977.[38] Later that year, the NRFM's attempt to pull off a national strike in support of the Firefighters' dispute also flopped.[39]

The downturn in industrial struggle was a serious blow to the SWP, although the extent of this problem was not immediately apparent, since it was disguised by the highly charged political environment in which it took place. The ideological radicalisation of the late 60s and early 70s had sufficient momentum to carry it forward beyond the collapse on the industrial front and it was nourished by the anger and bewilderment that was brewing under Labour. Disillusionment with life under a supposedly socialist government may not have prompted workers to resort to their most powerful weapon – industrial action – but it did bring to the surface an enormous number of discontents. A glance through the SWP's internal literature from the 1970s reveals a picture of intense political argument, including fierce polemics around various forms of oppression. Race, gender and sexuality became increasingly important in party propaganda and activity, and these emphases can be seen in the SWP's commitment to publishing two regular Asian language papers and separate magazines for women and blacks. Dedicated party sections were also set up, and organisers appointed, for various special-interest groups.[40]

In an attempt to bolster its flagging industrial perspective, but without losing its foothold in the union camp, the SWP instigated the Right To Work Campaign in October 1975.[41] This movement sought to champion the rights of growing numbers of jobless workers. But however much it hoped to rekindle a degree of militancy by working among the unemployed, the RTWC was essentially defensive and a symptom of the generalised malaise within the workers' movement.[42] Significantly, though, the RTWC signalled a shift in the SWP's perspectives, away from established union and political structures and towards the young working class, who were disproportionately represented amongst the unemployed and who, when they did find work, lacked a history of engagement with organised trade unionism.[43] This change in outlook was coupled with a highly contentious assessment of the state of the labour movement, which provoked furious faction fights and the biggest split in the history of the SWP. One of the assertions that lay at the heart of this argument was that many of those shop stewards who had formed the bedrock of the union rank and file had been undermined. One source of this weakening of shop floor organisation was the growing importance of full-time convenors, who largely replaced shop stewards in the policing of productivity deals. Another factor, according to Tony Cliff and other leading SWP members, was that many stewards had themselves been absorbed into the bureaucratic machine. This tendency to shift the balance of power in workplaces away from the rank and file and towards the trade union bureaucracy arguably helped to reaffirm the grip of reformism upon British workers.[44]

The SWP's shift in emphasis towards oppression and the young unemployed was confirmed when it was announced:

> [T]he twin themes of fighting racialism and fighting for the right to work now dominate our immediate perspectives for the next few months.[45]

For most of this period the SWP supposed that disenchantment with Labour would push a sizeable minority of the working class leftwards: one result of the anticipated increase in the popularity of left-wing ideas was the IS's decision to constitute itself as a fully fledged political party (the SWP) and to stand candidates in a number of parliamentary elections, with, to say the least, limited success. This change in tactics, which was encouraged by the growing threat from a fascist revival, was accompanied within SWP propaganda by an almost apocalyptic tone that echoed what the party believed to be (at least potentially) British capitalism's terminal crisis. In an article that announced the SWP's arrival as a party and which warned of the consequences of mass unemployment, Tony Cliff wrote:

> Under such conditions, two alternative policies will appear as a solution to this unemployment.
>
> One is the revolutionary socialist alternative – the overthrow of capitalism and the establishment of socialist planning. The other is the fascist solution . . .
>
> If, at the beginning of the revolutionary crisis, there is a mass revolutionary party of sorts, it can grow quickly in the months of the crisis so it is able to lead the working class to power.[46]

It is obvious now that British capitalism had more tricks up its sleeve than are suggested in these stark alternatives, but what is essential to grasp, for our purposes, is the importance the SWP now attached to the anti-fascist struggle. Rather than being a mere sideshow, the growing influence of the NF was felt to occupy centre stage in the fight for political hegemony. What the SWP's rhetoric may obscure, but which, with hindsight, is all too apparent, is that leaving the NF unchallenged would not only have entailed a failure to defend the targets of fascism from a crude and often brutal political creed; but it may also have given the far-right an opportunity to build the sort of mainstream political machine that the French Front National (FN) was able to establish during the 1980s. In its attempts to tackle resurgent fascism, however, the SWP faced a dilemma. On one hand the rise in racist attacks and the wider threat from the NF had to be addressed as a matter of urgency, but on the other, the party's lines of communication with the organised working class had been disrupted by the demise of the rank and file movement. The SWP was thus losing a lot of the influence it had once enjoyed amongst workers just at the time when an emergency presented itself.[47] There were, however, alternatives to hand, even if these were not immediately obvious.

As Trotskyists the SWP stood in a tradition of anti-fascism that did not shy away from the prospect of direct confrontation, even if this meant occasionally fighting in virtual isolation.[48] But the choice of tactics within a particular situation could be made only after assessing the state of the wider anti-racist and workers' movements and calculating the SWP's level of influence within this broader context. While the rank and file within the unions was still strong, and the NF relatively

feeble, the SWP's response could largely eschew street politics, in favour
of appeals to trade unions and organised workers. In 1974 the party
leadership sounded a cautious note:

> To be a serious threat, fascism requires mass unemployment, a ruined
> middle class and a demoralised ruling class, which is not what faces us at
> present.

And later:

> Our response must therefore be aimed not at mobilising 'public opinion'
> or individual acts of moral repugnance, but at activating the labour move-
> ment against the Front.[49]

A couple of years later the emphasis was subtly different, as the organisation realised that militant demonstrations were themselves a route
into important sections of the working class. By this time the RTWC
had become a major focus of SWP activity and the trade union movement in general had adopted a markedly more defensive stance; hence
this change in tone:

> Our policy of direct confrontation with the racialists has not only meant
> increased Socialist Worker sales, and increased recruitment to IS; it has
> also brought us into close contact with Asian organisations and especailly
> [sic] groups of young Asian workers.[50]

The following year, mass demonstrations against NF marches, first at
Wood Green and later in Lewisham, saw the SWP align itself with militant local blacks and Asians in physically resisting both marchers and
the police. The success of the Lewisham mobilisation in particular, both
in terms of neutralising the fascist street presence and locating the SWP
at the heart of a mass anti-racist movement, was not lost on the party's
leadership. The potential for building the SWP was becoming obvious.
As *Socialist Worker* editor, Chris Harman, put it in the week following
the Lewisham protest:

> There is a growing disillusionment with the Labour Government and there
> are two alternatives: towards the National Front or a socialist alternative.
> We are now recruiting about 150 people a month and less than a quarter
> of them are students. We are going to continue to grow in the months
> ahead.[51]

The Lewisham demonstration acted as the catalyst for founding the
ANL, but by that time RAR had been up and running for about a
year.

Rock Against Racism: origins and influences

The activists who initiated RAR were clearly not doing so from a position of political or organisational naivety. Red Saunders' letter to the music press, in calling for a *'rank and file* movement against the racist poison in rock music',[52] echoes the language of the workers' movement and reminds us of the socialist credentials of the letter's signatories. Roger Huddle's position as a designer in the *Socialist Worker* art room helps to confirm the close link between RAR and the SWP at this point. It is notable that he and Saunders were collaborating on plans for a one-off concert, to be called Rock Against Racism, and in conjunction with the RTWC, before the Clapton concert made such a splash.[53] Attempts to situate RAR within a wider politics of class can be seen in the campaign's frequent collaboration with the RTWC and the search for labour movement sponsorship for the London carnivals.[54]

The scale of the response to the letter was too sizeable to organise on anything but a highly devolved basis; in an act of frenetic delegation respondents might receive a reply announcing that they were now, say, 'RAR, Aberystwyth'.[55] As Red Saunders explains (with a touch of hyperbole):

> I mean talk about 'from the bottom up', it must have been the ultimate bottom up campaign. In fact it was so bottom up it didn't have a top.[56]

Although the SWP provided printing and office facilities, RAR designers, Syd Shelton and Ruth Gregory, insist these were not given free. Shelton declares that 'it was a straight commercial thing as far as the party officials were concerned'.[57] According to Shelton, RAR's main source of finance was the sale of literature and propaganda materials, especially badges and he estimates that one and a half million were sold over RAR's lifetime. Shelton explains the financial rationale in these terms: 'badges were the biggest money-spinner, because they cost fuck-all to make.'[58] But Roger Huddle disputes this interpretation, and he claims that the level of support given to RAR by the SWP must be understood as a product of political commitment, rather than pecuniary calculation. RAR's financial resources, he declares, were insufficient to finance the campaign's output of highly designed, printed publicity material: 'There was never any record of the amount of bromides used, images from SW files or any other materials. Any typesetting was not charged.'[59] At the very least, it seems evident that even if the SWP did not fund RAR directly, it failed to police its commercial dealings with the campaign terribly rigorously. The easy availability of art room equipment and consumables – including the expensive photographic paper that was used in abundance – and the fact that printing presses often over-ran by thousands of copies testify to this tolerant attitude. RAR's designers express considerable gratitude for such largesse, since it allowed them to experiment freely and to establish the movement's creative blend of words and images. Opinions differ over the extent to which this generosity was sanctioned by the party leadership, but it seems unlikely that such a substantial drain on resources was not monitored and permitted, at least by the party full-timers who ran the print-shop. Ian Birchall has suggested that a degree of managerial incompetence may have provided a significant loophole through which RAR's demands may have slipped unchecked,[60] but Huddle sees a more clearly political motive at work: 'By and large, because everyone involved was committed to the anti-Nazi struggle, and all at the printshop were revolutionary socialists, we were given the most extraordinary amount of help.'[61]

The amount of influence that the SWP exerted within RAR is a moot point. That prominent activists like David Widgery and Roger Huddle were party members suggests that the SWP's politics were well represented, but a number of other factors militate against the notion that RAR was held in a political headlock. For a start, none of the SWP members who were central to RAR held any leadership positions within the party and the extent to which Widgery, in particular, felt bound by party discipline is arguable.[62] Also, much of RAR's politics was the common currency of left-wing, and even liberal, circles. The SWP could claim no monopoly on anti-racism, anti-fascism, multiculturalism, anti-imperialism, the basic tenets of socialism, or practically any other aspect of the RAR message. In any case, the highly decentralised nature of the movement on the national level, and the diverse coalition of groups and individuals that it contained, would have made it difficult for the SWP to impose itself on all RAR's activities. Speaking in 2007, Red Saunders indicated the extent to which RAR was obliged to depend upon, and draw strength from, its scattered network of supporters, rather than transmitting directives from the campaign's London centre. Describing a typical plea for assistance from a RAR activist, who might ask, 'Well, can't you help me?' Saunders claims his response would likely be, 'No, we can't help you, I've got two rubber bands here, mate. You know, you've got to get on with it.'[63] It might be feasible, then, given the imbalance between RAR's scope and nature and the relatively slender means at the SWP's disposal, to attribute the party's relatively relaxed attitude towards RAR simply to the party's inability to effectively dominate such a wide movement. The contrast that Frith and Street detect, between Red Wedge's extreme centralism and RAR's profound federalism, may simply reflect a difference in size and bureaucratic reach between the Labour Party and SWP machines. To sustain this point of view, though, one would have to believe that the SWP's political emphasis on building 'socialism from below' had no organisational consequences and it would be difficult to reconcile with the party's lengthy history of participation in rank and file movements.

But whatever the underlying reasons, Frith and Street feel that 'RAR's most important achievement was to provide a model (and a name) for local activities that were put on without any reference to the central organization at all.'[64] Arguments certainly did arise between the different participants within RAR, but it is hard to find any compelling evidence of systematic political interference from the SWP. It is clear that suspicion towards both RAR and revolutionary socialists was fairly widespread, since many punks rejected any form of authority and significant numbers of black people distrusted what they regarded as the 'white' left.[65] But even so, attendance at a RAR gig imposed no political obligations on any acts or audience members, although it might offer an opportunity to make socialist propaganda. Even people who are decidedly cynical about the left, like Members vocalist and songwriter Nicky Tesco, concede that there was no attempt to impose a party line:

> We never had any . . . 'Commissar' turning up and basically trying to convert us, or anything like that. And also . . . you know, punk was renowned for its nihilism, which was . . . anathema to a lot of the hardcore Socialist Workers people.[66]

Those who were closest to RAR's centre confirm the tolerant attitude towards the organisation that prevailed within the SWP's headquarters, although some key figures attest to differences in attitude between the printshop's shopfloor workers and their more suspicious and wary political leadership. Although Syd Shelton worked closely with, and respected, individual members of the SWP, he views the party's enthusiasm for RAR more generally as essentially cosmetic, declaring that it participated in the movement as a mere 'fishing' exercise, through which it could hope to recruit new members.[67]

To gain an insight into the SWP's attitude to RAR, it is useful to examine the party's internal discussion documents. These offer a forum in which political perspectives are discussed with little need to make concessions to populism and public perceptions. With this in mind, what is particularly striking in the years following 1977 is that RAR rated scarcely a mention. Although the fight against racism was, as we have seen, an increasingly vital aspect of the party's work, RAR was not perceived as a key focus for its activity. Up until late 1977 the

RTWC acted as one of the main bearers of the SWP's anti-racist message, mainly because this opened a route into the workers' movement.[68] Local initiatives and demonstrations were also encouraged, but the ANL eventually provided the SWP's main point of entry into the anti-racist and anti-fascist milieu.[69] This bias towards the ANL is apparent throughout the SWP's literature, although popular music and RAR become more visible as one moves away from material destined for internal consumption and towards larger circulation journals. Thus, *Socialist Worker* gave popular music the highest profile,[70] while the monthly magazine, *Socialist Review*, paid it little attention in between carnivals. It is, of course, possible to attribute these variations in emphasis to the different functions and audiences of the publications in question. The weekly paper, especially in a time of political ferment, is given over largely to issues of organisation and agitation, and it is not an organ typically dedicated to lengthy articles that delve deeply into political theory. It is also the public face of the party and will be read well beyond the ranks of the subs-paying membership; as such it needs to connect immediately with the interests and preoccupations of a diverse readership. But still, RAR's virtual absence from the party's perspective documents and the stress that the SWP as a whole placed upon the ANL instead, requires an explanation.

If we wish to understand the divergent attitudes taken towards the ANL and RAR by the SWP, we need to appreciate the nature of each of the two campaigns – and especially their differences – and the SWP's political motivations. The first thing that needs to be stressed is that neither the ANL nor RAR can be termed a 'classic' united front. Trotsky endorsed the tactic partly because it offered a way for the revolutionary left to put pressure on the reformist leadership of the workers' movement, but this was clearly beyond the meagre resources commanded by the SWP. What was feasible, though, for the ANL, was to mobilise a broad spectrum of political forces, including significant sections of the organised working class, in opposition to the NF under the slogan, 'No platform for fascists'. The ANL was not simply an exercise in consciousness-raising; it was also, and very explicitly, a combat organisation. It strove to counter fascism through argument and, where necessary, direct confrontation. As such, the ANL attracted people on the understanding that they would be prepared to engage in activities that required a deeply felt commitment to the anti-fascist cause. This imperative to express and clarify one's political beliefs through 'a defining moment of joint activity'[71] is, as we have seen, a key component of the united front, but it was an impulse that was more sharply defined in the ANL than RAR. RAR gigs and discos may have provided opportunities for the organisation to proselytise and for the audience to explore, in practice, the connections between their aesthetic and political convictions, but attendance did not place a demand on the audience to subscribe to any of RAR's political beliefs. RAR's methods were more circumspect; they created cultural events which defied easy assimilation into a routine of passive consumption and political quiescence. RAR concerts were pregnant with the radical implications of multiculturalism and youth rebellion, and thus they segued easily into the overtly political carnivals that RAR organised jointly with the ANL. The audiences at RAR events may not necessarily have been activists in the sense that participants in street demonstrations were – although many will have shared an allegiance to both RAR and the ANL – but they were encouraged to draw practical conclusions from the implicitly anti-racist cultural practices in which they were engaged on a day-to-day basis. In light of our understanding of these differences between RAR and the ANL, we can make a judgement about the political natures of the two campaigns. Insofar as the united front is organised around a set of limited but explicit demands, with a broad appeal across the working class, it is clear that the ANL embodied such principles more clearly than RAR. The intensely political atmosphere of RAR events notwithstanding, it was the ANL that employed most rigorously what John Rees calls 'the united front method'.[72]

Given the politics of the SWP, we can understand why it supported campaigns that sought to exploit the potential of grassroots activism. For a party dedicated to the principle of proletarian self-emancipation, however, the ANL offered a more realistic vehicle for intervention among the working masses than did RAR. The semi-improvisational practices of RAR and the movement's narrow range of cultural enthusiasms had a limited appeal to most workers, especially older people, or to members of ethnic minorities. The ANL's simple anti-fascist message and structured organisation did not impose the same cultural barriers as RAR and it invited participation in ways that were familiar to most political activists. Unlike RAR, the ANL had a membership system and the kinds of formal arrangements through which trade unions and so on could register their affiliation. Many more people, including Holocaust survivors, could feel comfortable associating themselves with the ANL rather than RAR. Commenting upon RAR's working methods, Syd Shelton confirmed:

> It was anarchic . . . in the sense that nobody elected anyone to be on the RAR Committee. It was an organisation of activists. If you got your feet dirty and your hands dirty and rolled your sleeves up and got involved, that was it, that's all you did. There was no leader.[73]

Although RAR did maintain a loose scaffold of formal institutional structures, such as an elected national committee, activists confirm the spontaneity and flexibility of RAR's internal regime, which contrasted with the formality of a trade union conference, or even a formally constituted protest movement.[74]

We should add that the SWP's importance in providing ideological and logistical support for RAR was moderated by the experience of working alongside musicians and activists from a wide range of backgrounds. Many of the musical acts that performed regularly at RAR events were also closely involved in planning and organisation; thus Tom Robinson, Misty, Matumbi and Aswad all took leading roles in RAR.[75] The editorship of *Temporary Hoarding* was, significantly, in the hands of non-party activist and designer Ruth Gregory, and the presence of such people throughout the national network of local groups, as well as in key leading positions, counter-balanced SWP influence.[76]

It is apparent that a degree of cultural dissonance existed between RAR and certain elements within the SWP. This became manifest through *Socialist Review*'s coverage of the first carnival, which exposed a lack of understanding, on the part of some journalists, either of popular music or of RAR's brand of cultural politics. David Widgery and several other RAR members wrote a letter complaining of the magazine's '[a]trocious articles on Carnival',[77] and Roger Huddle contributed a piece criticising, among other things, the decision to invite two of the leading lights of Music for Socialism to write an article that, in his view, misunderstood both the intentions and the significance of RAR.[78] It is easy to sympathise with Huddle when reading John Rose's review of the carnival, in which he manages to misquote the lyrics of the Clash's most famous song and patronisingly declares that 'Rastafarianism is totally pessimistic about the black mans' [sic] future in Britain'. Rose concludes his foray into pop culture with the strangely worded claim that, 'We've won the first round in the struggle to talk the language of the generation of unemployables'.[79]

We should, however, beware of drawing too hard a line between RAR and the ANL, for many activists were involved across the board. As one Manchester-based socialist recalls, 'I was then an SWP member and the boundaries between ANL/RAR/SWP were very blurred'.[80] Apart from sharing many members and being motivated by similar politics, the two campaigns were mutually supportive. The large carnivals were joint affairs and the experience of putting 100,000 people onto the streets of London helped to establish the credibility of both wings of the movement. Within the trade unions, opposition to ANL affiliation was easier to overcome following the success of these massive shows of force.[81] The enormous numbers marching, rather than simply turning up for the music, indicated a level of political commitment that went beyond simple hedonism.[82]

Both Red Saunders and Roger Huddle are happy to concede that the ANL was, politically and numerically, the more significant partner in its relationship with RAR. Saunders stresses the two organisations' interdependence, though, when he says:

> I don't believe the ANL would have been half what it was without RAR . . . RAR wouldn't have been what it was without the ANL. It was a brilliant alliance.[83]

Summary

RAR was a product of complex political and social influences. The movement's relationship with the SWP was mediated through a set of political principles that were being applied during a period of dramatic change in outlook for the British left. The SWP's shift in emphasis, from industrial to political struggles, was one symptom of this and was one of the most important factors in shaping the party's relationship to RAR. The party's anti-Stalinist, humanist Marxism and the presence within its ranks of a number of young radicals, imbued with a commitment to cultural activism, were factors that shaped its ability to relate to a mass movement rooted in popular culture. The attempt to build a fruitful relationship between revolutionary politics and popular culture was not frictionless, however. It entailed a break with the typically distrustful attitude of most of the left towards 'Americanised' forms of mass culture, not to mention disputes between those members of the SWP who championed 'electric' rock and those for whom it represented unfamiliar (and perhaps even hostile) territory. It is clear, at any rate, that the SWP had strong reasons for seeking other channels through which to build its influence within the working class, hence its emphasis on the ANL and the RTWC. The virtual silence on the subject of RAR within the party's internal documents is a telling indication of the party's political priorities and their assessment of the position that RAR occupied within the wider anti-racist movement. The ANL provided a more secure bridge between party and class than did RAR and it partook more faithfully of the nature of the united front.

It is apparent that RAR should not be regarded as a simple SWP 'front' organisation, with little or no scope for autonomous activity. Not only is there considerable testimony confirming the lack of such overweening influence on the part of the SWP, but RAR's diffuse organisational structure also made rigid central control implausible. However, if RAR lacked the organisational and political homogeneity to allow it to be easily co-opted by the SWP, the party also had compelling political reasons not to seek such dominance over RAR. For the SWP to exercise a tight grip on the activities of a large and disparate body like RAR, it would have entailed accepting severe bureaucratic burdens with negligible political returns. An important part of the rationale for the united front tactic is, after all, to create conditions in which the influence of revolutionary politics can be extended beyond the existing constituency for socialist ideas. Building tightly controlled front organisations may appeal to the mind-set of those who confuse bureaucratic intrigue with politics, or it may obsess those for whom any attempt to promote socialism is tantamount to a Stalinist conspiracy, but it has little to offer people who wish to break out of the sectarian ghetto in which they have been hitherto confined. RAR had a powerful motive to take its message far beyond the pale of the organised left and the SWP had no interest in trying to thwart this mission.

Notes

1 Simon Reynolds, *Rip It Up And Start Again: Postpunk 1978–1984* (Faber & Faber, London, 2005), p. 179.
2 The name 'Socialist Workers Party' was adopted in 1977; before this the political tendency was known as the International Socialists. The IS grew from the Socialist Review Group, based around the journal *Socialist Review*, which began publication in 1950. In most instances, and following convention, I refer to the party in all its manifestations as the SWP, although when discussing the early history of the tendency I occasionally make specific reference to the IS. [A note for the punctuation-obsessed – the lack of an apostrophe to indicate the plural possessive in the word Workers is not a proof-reading error, but a stylistic choice on the part of the SWP.]
3 Sam Aaronovitch, 'The American threat to British culture', *Arena*, 2:8 (June/July 1951), pp. 3–22.
4 See: Hewlett Johnson, *The Socialist Sixth of the World* (Victor Gollancz, London, 1939).
5 Leon Trotsky, *Revolution Betrayed* (New Park, London, 1967).
6 Cited in: Robert Bideleux and Ian Jeffries, *A History of Eastern Europe* (Routledge, London, 1998), p. 531.
7 Accounts of this process can be found in: Bideleux and Jeffries, *Eastern Europe*, ch 19; Alex Callinicos, *Trotskyism* (Open University Press, Milton Keynes, 1990), ch 2; Gabriel Kolko, *The Politics of War: The world and United States foreign policy, 1943–1945* (Pantheon, New York, 1990 edition), chs 14–17; Marcel van der Linden, *Western Marxism and the Soviet Union: A survey of critical theories and debates since 1917* (Brill, Leiden and Boston, 2007).

8 Tony Cliff, *Trotskyism after Trotsky: The origins of the International Socialists* (Bookmarks, London, 1999), pp. 34–37.

9 For a comprehensive account of the theory of state capitalism, see Tony Cliff, *State Capitalism in Russia* (Pluto, London, 1974); for a condensed version see Callinicos, *Trotskyism*, ch 5.

10 The phrase is Ian Birchall's: Ian Birchall, interview (9 May 2001).

11 From the rules of the First International, cited in Karl Marx, 'Critique of the Gotha Programme', in Karl Marx and Frederick Engels, *Selected Works* (Lawrence and Wishart, London, 1968), p. 321.

12 Callinicos, *Trotskyism*, p. 79.

13 Karl Marx, *Economic and Philosophical Manuscripts of 1844* (Progress, Moscow, 1977 edition), p. 74.

14 Marx, *Economic and Philosophical Manuscripts*, pp. 70–71 (italics in original).

15 Quintin Hoare and Geoffrey Nowell Smith (eds), *Selections from the Prison Notebooks of Antonio Gramsci* (Lawrence and Wishart, London, 1971), p. 333.

16 Tony Cliff, *Lenin: Building the party* (Bookmarks, London, 1986), pp. 67–68.

17 Leon Trotsky, 'On the United Front', *The First Five Years of the Communist International, Volume Two* (New Park, London, 1974), p. 93.

18 Trotsky, 'On the United Front', p. 95.

19 For a discussion of the SWP's attitude towards the united front, see Renton, *When We Touched the Sky*, ch 6.

20 Leon Trotsky, *The Struggle Against Fascism in Germany* (Penguin, Middlesex, 1975), chs 5–8; Colin Sparks, *Never Again: The hows and whys of stopping fascism* (Bookmarks, London, 1980).

21 Communist policy during the Spanish Civil War is analysed in Felix Morrow, *Revolution and Counter-revolution in Spain* (New Park, London, 1976).

22 Some of the documents relating to this development can be found in Ken Coates and Tony Topham (eds), *Workers' Control: A book of readings and witnesses for workers' control* (Panther, London, 1970), section IV, chs 2 and 3.

23 Henry Phelps Brown, *The Origins of Trade Union Power* (Oxford University Press, Oxford, 1983), ch X.

24 John Kelly, *Trade Unions and Socialist Politics* (Verso, London, 1988), p. 105.

25 Kelly, *Trade Unions*, p. 107; Cliff and Gluckstein, *The Labour Party*, pp. 310–312.

26 Morgan, *People's Peace*, pp. 300–303.

27 Phelps Brown, *Origins*, ch XI.

28 Cliff and Gluckstein, *The Labour Party*, pp. 309–310. Kelly, *Trade Unions*, pp. 108–109.

29 For contrasting accounts of this period see: Jim Higgins, *More Years for the Locust: the origins of the SWP*, www.andyw.com/transfer/locust.pdf, downloaded 4 March 2008; and Ian Birchall, *Mass Party*. Higgins, a one-time

National Secretary of IS who was expelled in 1975, paints a much less inviting picture of IS and many of its leading members than does Birchall. Both men, however, defend the essential political principles upon which the group was founded, even if Higgins feels that these were later betrayed by a largely unaccountable leadership.

30 Birchall, *Mass Party*.
31 Higgins, *Locust*, p. 95.
32 Ted Crawford, 'A political appreciation of Tony Cliff and of his autobiography', *Revolutionary History*, 7:4 (2000), p. 190.
33 Childs, *Britain Since 1945*, p. 166.
34 Cliff, *World To Win*, pp. 112–113.
35 IS Internal Bulletin, April 1974, p. 10, *Alistair Mutch Papers*, Modern Records Centre, University of Warwick, MSS.284; Birchall, *Mass Party*; Kelly, *Trade Unions*, pp. 147–148.
36 IS Internal Bulletin, April 1974, p. 10.
37 Cliff, 'The balance of class forces'.
38 'Who doused the flame?', *Socialist Worker* (30 April 1977), p. 17.
39 Cliff, *World to Win*, p. 135.
40 For instance: IS Post-Conference Bulletin, 1975; IS Post-Conference Bulletin, 1976; SWP Pre-Conference Bulletin, No. 5, June 1977; SWP Pre-Conference Bulletin, No. 3, May 1978; SWP National Conference Bulletin (Resolutions), No. 5, 1978 all in *Alistair Mutch Papers*, Modern Records Centre, University of Warwick, MSS.284; see also Cliff, *World to Win*, p. 135.
41 Birchall, *Mass Party*.
42 Ibid.
43 This emphasis on youth was not completely unprecedented, however. Tony Cliff had argued in 1968 that the growing numbers of working class students in higher education presented opportunities for revolutionaries to link student struggles with the workers' movement. See: Ian Birchall, 'Seizing the time: Tony Cliff and 1968', *International Socialism Journal*, 2:118 (Spring 2008).
44 This dispute is discussed from a number of viewpoints in: Birchall, *Mass Party*; Cliff, *World to Win*, pp. 128–131; Crawford, 'Appreciation', pp. 190–192; Jim Higgins, 'Review of Tony Cliff: A World To Win', *Revolutionary History*, 7:4 (2000), pp. 218–220.
45 IS Post-Conference Bulletin, 1976, p. 3.
46 Tony Cliff, 'Why we need a Socialist Workers Party', *Socialist Worker* (8 January 1977), p. 10.
47 The tendency for anger to flow through political channels and street battles, rather than industrial disputes, was noted in Alex Callinicos, 'When the music stops', *Socialist Review* (June 1978), p. 15.
48 See, for instance, the editorial article 'Fists against fascists', *International Socialism Journal*, 1:10 (Autumn 1962).
49 IS Internal Bulletin, June 1974, p. 18, *Alistair Mutch Papers*, Modern Records Centre, University of Warwick, MSS.284.

50 IS Post-Conference Bulletin, 1976, p. 3; see also 'Our Anti-Fascist Work', IS Party Council Discussion Document, December 1976, *Stirling Smith Papers*, Modern Records Centre, University of Warwick, MSS.205.

51 David Pallister, 'So what if the vote is low? They mean to bust the system', *Guardian* (20 August 1977), p. 15.

52 *New Musical Express* (11 September 1976), p. 50 (my emphasis).

53 Red Saunders and Roger Huddle, interview (4 June 2000).

54 Garry Bushell, 'We have the right to work', *Sounds* (16 September 1978); Widgery, *Beating Time*, pp. 64, 70, 100–101. Ads were taken in the 'Carnival 2' programme (24 September 1978) by the NUM, CPSA, T&GWU, NUPE, *Socialist Worker*, *Morning Star*, ACTT, AUEW/TASS, *Labour Weekly* and SCPS, see 'Carnival 2 Programme', *Alistair Mutch Papers*, Modern Records Centre, University of Warwick, MSS.284.

55 Red Saunders and Roger Huddle, interview (4 June 2000).

56 Ibid.

57 Syd Shelton and Ruth Gregory, interview (16 May 2001).

58 Ibid.

59 Roger Huddle, personal communication (12 March 2008).

60 Red Saunders and Roger Huddle, interview (4 June 2000); Syd Shelton and Ruth Gregory, interview (16 May 2001); Ian Birchall, personal communication (2 September 2001).

61 Roger Huddle, personal communication (12 March 2008).

62 For Widgery's unwillingness to toe a strict party line see: Dave Renton, *The Poetics of Propaganda: David Widgery*, www.dkrenton.co.uk/anl/widgery. html, downloaded 9 November 2007. This point was also made in personal communications from: Roger Huddle (11 December 2000); Ian Birchall (4 September 2001).

63 *Rockin' Against Racism*, BBC Radio 4 (26 June 2007).

64 Frith and Street, 'Rock Against Racism and Red Wedge', p. 70.

65 Sabin, *Punk Rock: So What?*, pp. 206–207; Roger Sabin, personal communication (29 June 2001); Neil Spencer, 'I rebel poet' (Interview with Linton Johnson), *New Musical Express* (26 August 1978), pp. 25–26.

66 Nicky Tesco, interview (5 December 2000).

67 Syd Shelton and Ruth Gregory, interview (16 May 2001).

68 IS Post-Conference Bulletin, 1976, p. 3.

69 SWP Bulletin, No. 1, 1978, pp. 2–3, *Steve Jefferys Papers*, Modern Records Centre, University of Warwick, MSS.244; SWP National Conference Bulletin No. 5, 1978, pp. 8–9.

70 For a while in 1978 *Socialist Worker* adopted a decidedly populist tone in an attempt to relate more effectively with a readership drawn from the anti-racist movement. The so-called 'punk paper', as it became known in the SWP, reduced its emphasis on industrial struggles in order to devote more attention to general interest articles covering such things as sport, TV and music. This experiment in populism was shelved later in the year and, following the resignation of several journalists, Tony Cliff assumed editorial control. I am grateful to Ian Birchall for supplying details of this episode.

71 John Rees, interview (13 December 2000).
72 Ibid.
73 Syd Shelton and Ruth Gregory, interview (16 May 2001). This informality is also highlighted in my interview with Colin Fancy (2 April 2001).
74 Red Saunders and Roger Huddle, interview (4 June 2000); Roger Huddle, personal communication (11 December 2000); Widgery, *Beating Time*, p. 101; David Widgery, 'Beating Time – a reply to Ian Birchall', *International Socialism Journal* 2:35 (Summer 1987), p. 151.
75 Red Saunders and Roger Huddle, interview (4 June 2000); Renton, *When We Touched the Sky*, pp. 33–34.
76 Syd Shelton and Ruth Gregory, interview (16 May 2001).
77 Widgery, Gregory, Shelton and Huddle, 'Look Get it Straight', p. 14.
78 Roger Huddle, 'Hard rain', *Socialist Review* (July/August 1978), pp. 12–13.
79 John Rose, 'Rocking against racism', *Socialist Review* (June 1978), pp. 14–15.
80 Alastair Mutch, personal communication (21 February 2001).
81 Ian Birchall, interview (9 May 2001).
82 Red Saunders and Roger Huddle, interview (4 June 2000). See also Chris Salewicz, 'Carnival report', *New Musical Express* (6 May 1978), pp. 31–33. The article includes photographic evidence of the size of the march.
83 Red Saunders and Roger Huddle, interview (4 June 2000).

1 Utilising a reference to the Prince Far I album *Under Heavy Manners*, this cover of *Temporary Hoarding* dramatises the feeling among many anti-racists that they were in conflict with the forces of both the National Front and the British State.

2 A striking example of *Temporary Hoarding*'s sophisticated blend of photography, text and graphics. Influenced by punk design, but also early twentieth-century modernism and pop art, *Temporary Hoarding*, in Syd Shelton's words, was 'in a different category' to the amateur fanzines of the time.

p.m. Andy Dark

3 Just as the German artist and designer John Heartfield used montage to illustrate Hitler's links with big business, this image undercuts the reformist notion that the institutions of the state are politically neutral.

4 Rock Against Racism applied consistently high standards to all aspects of the campaign's visual identity, even down to this sheet of stickers.

a

The first Stevenage RAR record
Restricted Hours:
1. Getting Things Done   2.45 m
2. Still Living Out The Car Crash
                                (4.30m)
The Syndicate:
1. One Way Or Another   2.25m
2. I Want To Be Somebody   3.15 m

b

5a, 5b Stevenage RAR exemplified the marriage between political commitment, organisational skill and the do-it-yourself spirit of punk. Former activist Gareth Dent describes the techniques used in producing the packaging for the group's locally produced single: 'The cover was made with Letraset, images cut from magazines and bits typed on an IBM golfball typewriter – which was really high tech at the time. The singles were white labels, with the centres then rubber stamped.'

6 The creativity and initiative of local activists was a vital element in Rock Against Racism's success. This poster for Hull RAR was designed by Richard Lees and is based on a woodcut by the German expressionist Karl Schmidt-Rottluff.

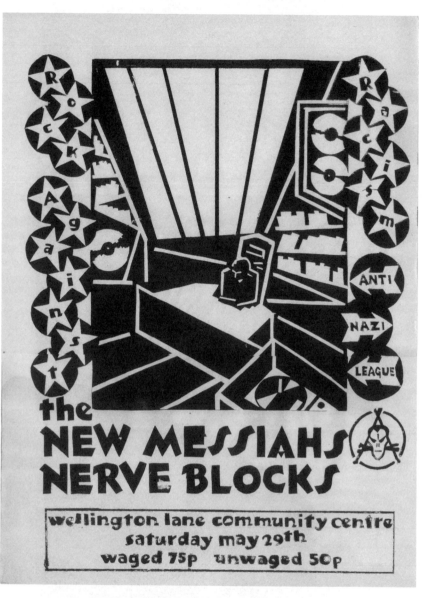

7 For this poster design, Richard Lees has reworked a woodblock print by American designer and artist Wharton Esherick.

a

b

8a, 8b Audiences at RAR gigs in Stevenage, 1979 – note the lack of stereotypical punks. The reality of the 'new music' scene in the provinces did not conform to the style guidelines laid down by the punk movement's London-based 'aristocracy'.

9 On the door in Stevenage, 1979. Just visible is a poster for Horace Ove's film, *Pressure*. Stevenage RAR was possibly unique in showing feature films.

4

Rock Against Racism, youth culture and multiculturalism

Some of the most vehement criticisms of RAR are concerned in one way or another with the organisation's cultural basis. Some critics, as we have seen, have drawn attention to the narrow cultural range that came to define RAR's activities, both in terms of the number of musical genres represented at concerts and the ethnic boundaries that were implicit in these choices. It has been argued that these limits were not, in some unproblematic way, an unavoidable by-product of a campaign that pursued essentially progressive political and cultural ends; rather, they represented a series of barriers which systematically excluded not only a multitude of musical genres but, more importantly, large sections of Britain's immigrant and ethnic minority populations. These are serious issues, but many of those who raise such criticisms have, in my opinion, failed to appreciate the social and cultural realities within which RAR was operating, and they show a poor grasp of the movement's politics. I would also argue (and this is crucial in discussing a grassroots campaign) that many commentators show little awareness of the practical problems encountered in launching and sustaining a protest movement. Translating political principles into effective action is not easy, and it may seem, for those of an overly academic or a sectarian bent,[1] rather a profane activity. I would maintain, however, that RAR displayed considerable sophistication and *chutzpah* in its work, although it is difficult to appreciate this if one views the matter from the level of an ivory tower.

If we are to clarify our understanding of RAR's mission, it is helpful to consider not only what RAR *was*, but also what it *was not*. RAR was, first and foremost, a direct response to racism within the British music industry. David Widgery explained that 'we chose pop music, not because of any illusions that it was intrinsically revolutionary, but because we knew the music on which the modern industry was based came specifically from the music of collective black resistance to racism and class exploitation'. He then went on to stress that, 'Having seized on this contradiction, we proceeded, like good agitators, to flog it to death'.[2] The cultural orbit within which RAR moved was, therefore, constrained in various ways. In general terms it exposed and exploited the patterns of ethnic influence that were implicit in the products of the pop music industry. This focus on the production and consumption of particular genres of popular music naturally excluded more than it included, and it could be argued it carried an implication that certain forms of culture were 'privileged' above others. But as Widgery makes plain, RAR did not, and never intended to, offer a platform for *all* culture. The agitator's need to find a point of leverage from which to exert influence over current events clearly motivated RAR's mission, but it also offers an insight into the dispute over RAR's attitude to the Asian community.

Insofar as Asian people shared an enthusiasm for rock music with their non-Asian friends and neighbours they could, and did, participate in RAR. The movement's activists thus point to the Southall carnival, the presence of large numbers of young Asians at gigs and the organisation's close relationship with Asian punk band Alien Kulture. They also stress RAR's strength in areas with large Asian populations, such as Leicester, Coventry, Birmingham, Southall and Bradford. West London RAR, which included Southall, had close links with local community groups the Indian Workers Association and the Southall Youth Movement. It also worked alongside the Peoples Unite movement, which brought together a disparate range of activists, including young Asian women who, according to Ruth Gregory and Syd Shelton, were protesting, amongst other things, at arranged marriages.[3] A report from Southall in the summer 1978 edition of *Temporary Hoarding* details some of the efforts local RAR organisers were making to build support in the area: 'RAR now has a Roots club every Thursday evening in the ballroom of the Indian Workers Association . . . Misty have got the whole thing going & with only grassroots word of mouth publicity there are already 2–300 people turning up each week.' Attempts to involve local cultural bodies in the staging of the Southall carnival were also being made: 'RAR is working with a number of other local labour and cultural groups to combine music[,] drama and dance for a great anti-racist festival.'[4] Such political and social connections were doubly important because of the absence, in the 1970s, of a popular-cultural bridge between Asian and white British youth. The bhangra phenomenon was confined, by choice and happenstance, to Asian communities[5] and the artists who were to develop today's forms of Asian-inflected popular music, and who were to create a new musical vocabulary, were yet to become active in 1977. This was not a development that RAR could have anticipated or pre-empted through an act of political will.

In contrast to the relatively slender popular-cultural links between Asian and white British youth, one must appreciate the lengthy cross-cultural exchanges that had taken place between Afro-Caribbean artists and white British audiences and performers in the post-war period. In the 1950s and 1960s Britain's popular music scene came under the influence of Caribbean talents as diverse as Winifred Atwell, Emile Ford and the Checkmates, and Desmond Dekker. These and similar examples lend weight to Dick Hebdige's previously cited speculations regarding the importance of immigrant communities in the development of British youth culture; but they also help to define the ethnic limits within which that process operated. However regrettable it may be, no comparable process of integration occurred regarding Asian music.

Before leaving the subject of Asians and RAR, we must bear in mind that RAR events were not simply platforms for youth subcultures; they were also collective expressions of political sentiments with which a wide variety of people could empathise. Whatever negative connotations attached themselves to punk rock – and film director Gurinder Chadha remembers her own assumption that punk was a 'hard' and predominantly right-wing phenomenon[6] – RAR and the ANL formed a pole of attraction for individuals who wanted to express their opposition to racism and the NF. The 'offputting effect' identified by Frith and Street may not have been entirely absent, then, but it was offset by a feeling of empowerment that was becoming increasingly strong within Asian communities. Chadha, for instance, attended the first RAR carnival by herself (she told her parents she was going shopping in Croydon). Fearing the threat of far-right violence she did not go on the march beforehand, but went straight to Victoria Park. She recalls her 'sense of immense relief' as a 'sea of people with banners', most of whom were white, entered the park. Far from feeling excluded, Chadha emphasises the happiness she felt as she realised that the NF did not represent the opinions of most white people. This positive message was conveyed to her family when they saw the photographs of the enormous carnival crowd in the music press.[7] Ausaf Abbas, ex-bassist with Alien Kulture, recalls feeling 'very included' through the RAR experience. Abbas took the unusual route of forming a predominantly Pakistani punk band, and he notes how groups like the Clash set an example of cross-cultural co-operation that helped to demonstrate the possibility of developing culturally eclectic approaches to popular music. He remembers the mid-1970s as a time when Asian British youth did not have a youth culture of their own 'to cling to', but also as a period when Asians began to become more self-assured, both individually and collectively.[8] Both he and Gurinder Chadha cite the anti-NF demonstration in Southall on 23 April 1979 as a major turning point in this process. Abbas and Chadha each had to overcome parental opposition to their potentially risky political activities – and for Chadha her experience at the RAR carnival marked the start of a period during which she became very politically active – but they both agree that RAR helped to establish the conditions for a more self-confident and assertive mood within Asian communities across the UK.[9]

RAR made tactical choices about which musical styles showed the most potential for radical political expression. Given the state of popular music in the mid-1970s, it should not surprise us that the schisms that had opened up within and between various genres at this time were replicated within RAR. Thus progressive rock, heavy metal and disco were either excluded or marginalised, whilst punk and reggae took centre stage. It is in this context that we need to scrutinise Frith and Street's claim that these latter styles embodied, for RAR, a kind of proletarian 'authenticity'. It is apparent that this statement does not refer in some simplistic way to the working class origins of punk and reggae performers, for these are indistinguishable from the backgrounds of equivalent artists from other genres. Rather, Frith and Street maintain, 'it is clear in retrospect that conventional political assumptions determined tastes'.[10] In other words, RAR's ideological presuppositions led the movement's organisers to impute to punk and reggae a kind of 'correctness' that they denied to musical forms with equally valid proletarian credentials. But this argument tends to down-play the very real differences between musical genres in the 1970s, differences that were immanent, rather than imposed from without by socialist ideologues. It is true that punk (being almost entirely 'white') and reggae (being almost entirely 'black') became emblematic of the racial solidarity promoted by RAR, but it is also true that they both displayed a political potential that was hard to detect in much of the rest of the music industry at the time. However much one may express a personal preference for disco, heavy metal or 'prog rock', it is disin-genuous to suggest that the themes of hedonism, gothic fantasy and unworldly romanticism with which these styles were identified could have delivered the political punch of punk and reggae. This is not to say that either of these latter styles was inherently 'progressive'. Punk, for instance, was highly contradictory and RAR's intervention was partly intended to counter right-wing influences. Some have also claimed that Rastafarianism expressed a level of misogyny that could be troubling for the constituencies to which RAR appealed. What is indisputable, though, is that by 1975 many people had concluded that popular music needed to be purged of the self-indulgent excesses of multi-millionaire stars and bombastic 'stadium rock'. Punk and reggae offered refreshingly down to earth, sometimes amateurish, alternatives that frequently explored issues such as personal and group identity, alienation, oppression and exploitation: themes which were essential to RAR's politics.

The punk connection

Paul Gilroy contends that punk supplied 'an oppositional language through which RAR anti-racism could speak a truly populist politics'.[11] In making this point, Gilroy touches on the concerns of people like David Widgery, who warned that the left needed to constantly prove its relevance to people who felt little or no affinity with the venerable traditions of the British labour movement. RAR's pioneers were certainly keen to advance this aim through the medium of popular music, but it is equally clear that they came to the project without a clear blueprint. It was not obvious that punk, for instance, would prove so crucial to RAR's success. Although the 'black band plus white band' formula was arrived at very quickly and reggae was part of the mix from the very beginning, RAR's original organisers had no direct link with the punk circuit and the concert line-ups reflected their own experience and enthusiasms. As Roger Huddle explains: 'RAR started off as a kind of retrospective – soul, funk, pub rock – 'cause that's what we thought we could do. That was the prevailing independent music, away from the big pop stars.'[12]

Punk and reggae double bills became the norm towards the end of 1976, following a process of experimentation, calculation and accident. A gig at the Roundhouse, in London, featuring reggae band Aswad, and all-female punk act the Slits, alerted RAR to the latent synergy between these two forms of music. The dissident status of punk became confirmed with the infamous confrontation between Bill Grundy and the Sex Pistols, on the *Today* TV programme. This spectacle, in which the Pistols, along with members of their entourage, ridiculed the bemused Grundy and swore their way onto the tabloids' front pages, encouraged Roger Huddle and Red Saunders to present punk rock as an important part of RAR's critical package. As Huddle explains: 'We both understood that there was a shift and if we didn't orientate on that, then we would miss the audience . . . It was our experience politically, that we just knew that something was happening and the next gig had to be a punk band and a reggae band.'[13]

RAR's initial approach to punk, then, was conditioned by a perception that it possessed a radical energy that could be tapped by the anti-
racist movement. This was partly down to punk's assault on the
ideological assumptions behind studio-bound rock and pop and the
bloated pretensions of so many 'stadium bands' and 'progressive rock'
musicians. Many punks rejected self-indulgent technical virtuosity,
disavowed the themes of most youth-oriented music and attempted to
minimise the gap between audience and performer, and they thereby
raised the possibility of reconfiguring the deeply ingrained habits
of musical production and consumption. An emerging network of
independent labels and record stores, and a growing underground of
amateur fanzines, began to define the new movement's parameters.
Dave Laing makes the point that: 'Unlike nearly every other youth
subculture . . . punk began as music and punks themselves began as
music fans and performers. In every other case, the youth adopted an
already existing type of music.'[14]

It can be argued that punk represented a practical critique of the
music industry at the point of production. Laing makes a connection
with the ideas of Walter Benjamin, for whom the 'message or content
of a work of art' did not exhaust its political significance, and according
to whom one also needs to examine 'the function of a work within
the literary *production relations* of its time'.[15] Punk seemed to embody
an attitude that rejected the standardised production and passive consumption of popular music and extended the promise of a critical
audience to whom RAR could address its arguments. We might also
add that some of the rituals and practices associated with the punk
phenomenon at the level of the consumer reinforced this impression of
a critically engaged movement, representing as they did attempts to
efface the distinction between performer and audience and to strip
away some of the elitist pretensions of musical forms such as disco. The
punk habit of spitting at bands, for instance, can be interpreted in
numerous ways, but at one level it seemed to represent a way of sullying
the mystique of the musician, or at least demonstrating the audience's
distrust of (or resentment towards) artistic authority. Punk dances
like the pogo, in which audience members would leap up and down on
the spot, or crash into one another with little control or co-ordination,
can be set against the intricate and highly stylised movements of disco.
One of the things that distinguished punk from so many other musical
forms was its emphasis on the immediate; upon live performance in
intimate venues, rather than heavily stage-managed spectacles in massive
stadiums; upon the two- or three-minute single, rather than the
interminable concept album. The visceral and experiential aspects of

punk rock have been explored in the work of Ben Watson and Esther Leslie, two of the genre's most perceptive and enthusiastic advocates, who note how the movement challenged the ideological assumptions behind most popular music, through its own articulation of an 'anti-commodity populism'.[16]

But if punk carried a radical charge, we should take care not to accept at face value all of the myths that have been circulated in its name. Our vision of punk is highly selective and is often shaped by media representations of the dress codes, attitudes and pronouncements of a small coterie of London-based innovators, such as Sex Pistols manager Malcolm McLaren and graphic designer Jamie Reid. Provincial manifestations of punk style – whether derivatives of, or deviations from, the media-hyped archetypes that have come to dominate histories of punk – may seem inauthentic or devalued in comparison with them. But some commentators have questioned the validity of this top-down perspective and have reasserted the importance of regional attempts to articulate the DIY spirit of punk, for instance through exploiting locally available resources like second-hand shops and sympathetic music venues.[17] Commenting on Dick Hebdige's highly influential analysis of the subculture, Gary Clarke notes:

> This metropolitan centeredness contradicts Hebdige's emphasis on working-class creativity, since most of the punk creations that are discussed were developed among the art-school avant-garde, rather than emanating 'from the dance halls and housing estates.' Hebdige's vision of punk is extremely elitist; despite punk's proletarian stance (constantly emphasized), his concern is typically for the 'art' of the innovators[.][18]

In a similar vein, Helen Reddington cautions against accepting without question what are 'often personal and metrocentric' histories of punk rock, including 'Jon Savage's *England's Dreaming* to Malcolm McLaren's many versions of events (in particular his film *The Great Rock 'n' Roll Swindle*) in which he is the star and everyone else supporting players'.[19]

But if punk as a visual style was far more disparate and diffuse than might be supposed from an examination of the self-consciously spectacular productions of the movement's London-based 'aristocracy', it should also be apparent that the subculture should not be associated exclusively with the political proclivities of these same leading figures. It can be claimed, for instance, that punk's subversive reworking of symbols of authority such as the union flag or images of the Queen, represented an assault on the ideological sensibilities of the British establishment and that these elevated the critical aesthetics of punk rock above the realm of 'conventional' politics: it is at this point that reference is often made to certain individuals' dedication to the anarchist ideals of the Situationist International. However, to maintain this interpretation requires that we place too much emphasis on the highly individualistic politics of a small elite. Just as punk style in the provinces developed in ways that suited local interests, so the everyday concerns of ordinary young people – racism, women's oppression, unemployment, homelessness and so on – featured heavily in the music. Responses to these pressures would not be confined to the types of symbolic revolt that we have become accustomed to identifying as typically 'punk'. Like it or not, the same conditions that stimulated the growth of rebellious subcultures were also stirring up forces with reactionary agendas, and these were less likely to be deterred by the playful sloganeering of Situationist anarchism than they would the more 'conventional' weapons of anti-fascist propaganda and direct confrontation. As we shall see, those National Front ideologues who attempted to reach out to punk rockers were perfectly willing to take 'ironic' references to race and Nazi insignia at face value, and to use any opportunity that presented itself to celebrate public displays of symbols of race hatred such as the swastika. Any attempt to understand the politics of punk rock must take into account not only the intentions of the movement's most prominent and vocal spokespeople, but also the rather less carefully contrived ways in which social antagonisms were played out among young people in a multitude of local situations. We must also recognise that an influential and highly vocal stratum of the punk milieu was resolutely petit-bourgeois – the record shop owners, the managers, the independent label bosses, even, to some extent, the bands, occupied a social position that does not coincide with the 'punk-as-proletarian' stereotype.[20] Indeed, the presence of so many aspiring entrepreneurs among punk's ranks may help to explain why anarchism, a quintessentially petit-bourgeois political creed, gained such a high profile in the movement's early days, particularly among its London-based avant-garde.[21] Despite the hotly contested claims that punk drew inspiration from the politics of the Situationist International, the nakedly commercial ambitions of some of the genre's founding figures, Malcolm McLaren included, tend to undercut high-minded appeals to political principle.

Commenting upon punk rock's ties to the pre-existing machinery of cultural production, and in criticism of what he saw as David Widgery's tendency to underestimate the constraints this imposed on the genre, Ian Birchall notes:

There is a framework in which popular music is produced and marketed
... punk attempted to escape from some of those things, but was fairly
rapidly co-opted ... I don't think it was possible for any of the punks
to ... simply maintain, by personal integrity, their independence from that
process.[22]

A number of punk artists achieved considerable commercial success and
the concert circuit that RAR established was instrumental in spreading
punk's influence on a national scale.[23] For some bands, playing RAR
gigs presented an opportunity to gain important exposure and credibility and in certain cases this provided an added incentive to identify with
the movement.[24] RAR also paid its acts, which was not insignificant for
struggling bands, although the sums were modest and were constrained
by RAR's policy of making entrance to its gigs cheap or free.[25] We
should be aware, too, that some acts, such as Misty In Roots, displayed
considerable political commitment and almost certainly sacrificed lucra-
tive engagements in favour of badly paid RAR concerts.[26] For successful
acts like Elvis Costello and the Attractions, and the Clash, there could
have been no immediate financial motive behind their support for
RAR, although several commentators have indicated that some band
managers were prone to a level of self-interested cynicism that the acts
themselves rarely displayed.[27]

RAR's emphasis on the punk rock subculture was partly pragmatic;
it stemmed from the recognition that the campaign needed to use the
'tools' to hand and had alighted on the sharpest instrument available.
This much is clear from Roger Huddle's comments on the matter. But
I have also indicated that a debate had opened up within punk regarding
the use of symbols such as the swastika. Various commentators have
suggested that this had more to do with upsetting the older generation
than proving any sympathy with fascist politics.[28] However, some of
those I have spoken with testified to the licence that such attitudes gave
to racists. One ex-member of the Young National Front (YNF) declared
that the 'Sex Pistols legitimised the swastika', and explained how punk
rock made it possible for him to go out in public wearing nationalist
symbols, as long as these were integrated into a punk ensemble of
mohair jumper and drainpipe trousers.[29] He also recalled YNF discos
at which people would seize upon any lyrical reference to the racist
right as a pretext for communal chanting. In this context the Clash's
White Riot presents an obvious example, but even the phrase 'too many
right-wing meetings', in the Jam's song, *Down in the Tube Station
at Midnight*, could provoke such a response.[30] The fact that such
cultural parasitism could provide a bond between members of fascist

organisations suggests that the right's search for unifying aesthetic and symbolic themes should not be taken lightly. We can see this process at work in the NF's literature. For instance *Bulldog*, the paper of the YNF, carried a Rock Against Communism (RAC) supplement from issue number 16 onwards, but this was a fairly straightforward exercise in cultural subterfuge, largely concerned with reporting YNF attendance at concerts that were unconnected with the Front, in an attempt to appropriate them for itself.[31] A few RAC gigs were arranged, but these were often ill-organised affairs, which faced the threat of disruption by anti-fascists. Ironically, even the top ten song list published regularly in the National Front's literature proved 'impossible to sustain . . . without naming such acts as the Clash and Sham 69, even though they knew these bands were their mortal enemies'.[32] The dreary cultural vacuum that prompted such a desperate longing for relevance was evoked by one young skinhead, writing for *Temporary Hoarding*:

> [S]kinheads, not the punk spillover of now, but the real thing . . . hated hippies, pretended to hate blacks, and were desperate for some positive ideology to give the movement permanence.
> None came – we never had any heroes, no movies to attach ourselves to, not even our own music – we nicked reggae from the blacks.[33]

The contention of critics like Jon Savage that RAR's intervention undermined punk's radical discourse must be set against evidence from other sources which attests to the corrosive influence of the subculture's forays into the territory of fascism. What seemed like a daring (and sometimes profitable) flirtation with Nazi chic could look very different when viewed from the racist fringe.[34] It should also be appreciated how implausible it was to reconcile a fascination with the imagery of the Third Reich with the project of building an anti-racist coalition that could reach out to people who were obvious targets of right-wing hatred, such as Jews, blacks, gays, socialists and trade unionists.[35]

It is clear from the history of bands like Skrewdriver, who aligned themselves with fascist politics, and the evident preoccupations of the YNF, as expressed through the pages of *Bulldog*, that punk and new wave music were seen as channels through which British Nazism could proselytise and recruit.[36] To this extent, then, the struggle for influence among white youth was to be fought upon terrain already chosen by the right, rather than marked out by RAR. The Nazi contention that punk rock was a 'white folk music' needed to be countered. RAR's attempt to deny a safe haven to racists and fascists within popular culture is analogous to the intention, on the part of the ANL and others, to deny them the freedom to mobilise on the streets. This tactic is in accord with the Trotskyist analysis of fascism, which sees it searching for forms in which to manifest itself that compensate for the movement's lack of a strong base within the organised working class or the big battalions of capital.

The black culture connection

A natural fit between punk and reggae is claimed by a number of authorities and a strong 'dub' element is clearly evident within the music of white acts like the Clash, Elvis Costello, the Ruts and the Members. Nicky Tesco reiterates the point that reggae was often the music of choice for young people who were weary of the existing music scene and looking for a more challenging and interesting alternative. He also confirms Lloyd Bradley's observation that reggae filled a gap left by the scarcity of punk product: 'We didn't have punk records to play, they just weren't there in any kind of abundance, so . . . most of the people spinning would be playing, like, reggae cuts and stuff like that.'[37]

Preceding these developments was a sometimes contradictory relationship between black and white youth, mediated through the medium of reggae. Although these subcultural transactions imply a degree of street-level integration, the manner in which chauvinistic skinheads could forge an identity from a mixture of English and Jamaican influences alerts us to the fact that even the most unlikely musical and stylistic phenomena can be appropriated by the right.[38] The emergence of a new generation of ska bands, often mixed-race, that took place in the late 1970s and early 1980s was a positive advance, but the fringe of racists who latched onto some acts confirms that black culture itself was contested between all sides in racial politics. NF disc jockeys, after all, could hardly enthuse the young master race with the military marches that John Tyndall favoured, so black music constituted the core of their repertoire.[39] As with punk, then, RAR's attitude towards reggae was not simply a positive affirmation of the genre's radical potential; it also has to be viewed as an attempt to build a cultural coalition in an area vulnerable to incursions from the far-right. These contradictory cultural interactions help us to understand the importance of the anti-racist multiculturalism that RAR addressed to white youth.[40]

Another determinant of RAR's relationship with black culture was the part that reggae played in the conflict between Britain's Anglo-Caribbean population and the state.[41] Red Saunders and Roger Huddle were sensitive to reggae's political dimensions, particularly through its association with the Notting Hill Carnival. The Metropolitan Police were heavily implicated in the violence that had exploded at the event

in 1976 and a number of raids on music clubs, often under the pretext
of searching for drugs, seemed to signal an attempt on the part of the
state to police the free expression of Anglo-Caribbean culture.[42] These
pressures helped to mark out reggae as an oppositional form and to
promote the emergence of a militant, hard-edged UK reggae sound.[43]
The official reason given for state repression within black, mainly Anglo-
Caribbean, communities was a concern over law and order. Mugging
panics and street crime became coded justifications for draconian policing and surveillance.[44]

The importance of this moment in the fortunes of British punk rock
needs to be appreciated. Members of one of the most influential bands
of the time, the Clash, were present at the Notting Hill riot and not
only did the experience help to consolidate some pre-existing antipa-
thies towards the British state and police – 'We all hated the police',
declares one of the group's entourage: 'There was an unspoken understanding that they were on the opposing side'[45] – but it also led the band
to explore reggae as an explicitly rebellious and dynamic musical form.
One of the Clash's biographers, Marcus Grey, describes the process:

> The Clash camp began to see reggae culture as a blueprint for the develop-
> ment of both their own music and of punk in general. The punk scene,
> still largely an elite club for art school students and decadent poseurs,
> could be co-opted for the disaffected white equivalent of the rioting black
> youths; and could provide a more positive politicisation process than that
> offered by the National Front. [46]

Reggae's pedigree as a form of counter-cultural dissent is confirmed
by rock journalist Caroline Coon, who observes that, in the pre-punk
period, 'reggae carried the torch of protest that white rock music had
had in the late 1960s but then lost'.[47] Reggae, and the associated religious philosophy of Rastafarianism, was an important channel through
which an often-embattled Caribbean diaspora could articulate its concerns. The sense, so strong in many reggae songs, of a looming apoca-
lypse, and of the corruption and decadence running through British
society, found plenty of purchase on the minds of punk rockers and it
helps to define what novelist Jonathan Coe calls the 'ungodly strange-
ness' of the 1970s.[48] In the metaphorical language and aural qualities
of 'heavy' reggae, both white and black youths found a peculiarly powerful means of expressing their anger and alienation, so when the Ruts
– a notable punk act of the time – sang 'Babylon's Burning', they were
adding another link in a chain of cultural associations that bound
together young people across racial and ethnic divides.

Given these connections, I would suggest that Notting Hill, rather than the hippy festivals of the 1960s and early 1970s, was the most important influence on RAR's decision to utilise the carnival format for its mass events.[49] Although the influence of the 1960s was apparent in the, sometimes surreal, iconography and intentions of RAR carnivals,[50] the idea of registering a protest through a massive, celebratory, street procession and music festival has obvious affinities with Caribbean traditions.[51] This overtly spectacular form segued neatly with the more prosaic intention to put on a show of force that the racist right would be incapable of matching.[52]

Locating RAR within a particular historical moment, and appreciating the overlapping social, cultural and political contexts within which the organisation was operating, helps us to assess more rigorously those criticisms of RAR which focus on the organisation's cultural biases. Given the opportunities available to RAR's founders, and the constraints under which they worked, their approach to multiculturalism seems more akin to the 'critical' variety identified by C.W. Watson, than the easy celebration of 'difference' so often associated with the multiculturalist project. Watson cites Terence Turner's definition of critical multiculturalism as an attempt 'to use cultural diversity as a basis for challenging, revising and relativizing basic notions and principles common to dominant and minority cultures alike, so as to construct a more vital, open and democratic common culture'.[53]

Despite all of the above, and although a strong affinity for black music clearly motivated many of RAR's white supporters, it is clear that not all young people felt the same deep cultural attachment. The music they enjoyed may have grown from seeds sown in black people's experience, but this did not necessarily translate into enthusiasm for dub reggae or delta blues. It would be mistaken to infer that this lack of interest in listening to black music barred such fans from adopting a principled anti-racist political position. As one rank and file RAR activist declares: 'I wasn't a big black music fan at all. I got into reggae a little bit, but not a great deal ... I was more into the Clash playing reggae than anyone else.'[54] The same person also made the point that RAR had a limited appeal for black youth. As a local organiser his main experience of RAR was through the small local gigs that were RAR's mainstay: 'I don't believe that millions of black kids came to the gigs, I mean I was at the gigs. The sound system would bring in 15 mates, all carrying a record, saying they were roadies ... They didn't bring in lots of black kids, but they brought in lots of white punk fans who then listened to reggae.'[55]

The point, however, was that RAR's main aim was not to attract a large black reggae audience, but to 'attack, within the *white* working class, the racism that was brewing up'.[56] This theme has been reiterated by RAR personnel on numerous occasions. Syd Shelton points to the NF's attempts to recruit among punk fans at a time when a great deal of political ambiguity surrounded the movement. He states: 'The problem was not a black problem or an Asian problem, the problem was a white problem. They were the people whose minds we had to change – white youth, not black youth.'[57]

Summary

The youth cultures with which RAR most closely identified were contested between political tendencies and music industry interests before RAR appeared on the scene. Punk had emerged as a significant, if somewhat ambivalent, radical phenomenon in its own right and reggae was implicated in the politico-cultural struggles between black people and the British state. Furthermore, it is clear from the testimony from the far-right that black culture was not immune to co-option by forces opposed to the kind of multiculturalism that RAR espoused. Under these circumstances it would be naive to expect the left to adopt a neutral attitude towards popular culture, although RAR's response was clearly not the only one available. Far from representing the imposition of a unitary Marxist aesthetic upon the field of popular culture, RAR was the product of a particular set of political ideas, being applied in specific circumstances, by a group of people who shared a number of ideological, if not necessarily organisational, affiliations.

In the first instance RAR began as a reaction, rather than a stimulus, to events. Like all small agitational groups it needed to gain some social leverage and to this end it chose a route to mass appeal that combined an awareness of the political potential that was building around certain musical genres and an appreciation of their relative popularity. RAR's major polemical point, that a streak of racism ran through the music industry, provided an organisational focus for the movement as well as a cultural boundary. On the one hand this imposed certain restrictions on RAR's repertoire and appeal, but on the other it mobilised the genuine enthusiasms of many thousands of young people, for whom black-influenced music was an important part of life. If RAR were simply a cultural ginger group, hoping to disseminate and popularise as wide a range of music as possible, from the greatest variety of backgrounds, then its limitations might seem arbitrary and perverse. However, as a campaign dedicated to mobilising thousands of young people in defence of an anti-racist message, it showed considerable finesse in its political and cultural calculations.

Notes

1 I am not using the word 'sectarian' to refer to an unwillingness to tolerate opposing viewpoints, but rather in the sense Marx and Engels use the word in the *Communist Manifesto*, to describe a tendency for some individuals and political groups to hold themselves aloof from active engagement with workers.
2 Widgery, 'A Reply', p. 150.
3 Syd Shelton and Ruth Gregory, interview (16 May 2001). Although the phrase used by the interviewees was 'arranged marriages', it is possible that the target of this campaign will have been *forced* marriages, which are a different matter altogether.
4 *Temporary Hoarding*, No. 6 (Summer 1978).
5 John Hutnyk acknowledges as much in his critique of RAR, although he takes the organisation to task for not doing more to build bridges to the Asian community: John Hutnyk, *Critique of Exotica: Music, politics and the culture industry* (Pluto Press, London, 2000), p. 156.
6 Gurinder Chadha, interview (26 March 2008).
7 Ibid.
8 Ausaf Abbas, interview (23 March 2008).
9 Gurinder Chadha, interview (26 March 2008); Ausaf Abbas, interview (23 March 2008).
10 Frith and Street, *Rock Against Racism and Red Wedge*, p. 76.
11 Gilroy, *There Ain't No Black*, p. 121.
12 Red Saunders and Roger Huddle, interview (4 June 2000).
13 Ibid.
14 Laing, *One Chord Wonders*, p. xi. Ian Birchall argues that we should not push the idea of punk's discontinuity too far, however, since many punk bands drew heavily on earlier precedents. He cites the Sex Pistols' debt to Eddie Cochran as an example: Ian Birchall, personal communication (28 February 2008).
15 Walter Benjamin, 'Understanding Brecht', cited in Laing, *One Chord Wonders*, p. 127 (my italics).
16 Esther Leslie and Ben Watson (2001), *The Punk Paper: A Dialogue*, www.militantesthetix.co.uk/punk/Punkcomb.html, downloaded 25 May 2006.
17 Frank Cartledge, 'Distress to impress?: local punk fashion and commodity exchange', in Sabin, *Punk Rock: So What?*.
18 Gary Clarke, 'Defending ski-jumpers: a critique of theories of youth subcultures', in Simon Frith and Andrew Goodwin (eds), *On Record: Rock, pop and the written word* (Routledge, London, 1990), p. 72.
19 Helen Reddington, *The Lost Women of Rock Music: Female musicians of the punk era* (Ashgate, Aldershot, 2007), p. 1.

20 Savage, *England's Dreaming*, pp. 416–418.
21 Pursuing this line of argument we might also draw attention to those analyses of fascism, including Trotsky's, which locate its social roots among the petit-bourgeoisie: a perspective that may lead us to redefine punk's middle-class, metropolitan elite as a potential weak link in the subculture's encounter with the NF, rather than a guarantor of the movement's anti-authoritarianism. Such suggestions are, I would acknowledge, highly speculative.
22 Ian Birchall, interview (9 May 2001).
23 Savage, *England's Dreaming*, pp. 484–485, p. 516.
24 Nicky Tesco, interview (5 December 2000); Colin Fancy, interview (2 April 2001); Sabin, *Punk Rock: So What?*, p. 206.
25 Nicky Tesco, interview (5 December 2000); Syd Shelton and Ruth Gregory, interview (16 May 2001); *Temporary Hoarding*, No. 7 (Winter 1979), p. 22.
26 *Temporary Hoarding*, No. 7 (Winter 1979), p. 22.
27 Red Saunders and Roger Huddle, interview (4 June 2000); Widgery, *Beating Time*, pp. 94–5; Stewart Home, *We Mean It Man*.
28 My personal experience of punk confirms this interpretation. My friends and I would often mock our parents' generation's frequent invocations of 'The War', which generally preceded a lecture on how easy our lives were. Also, Ian Birchall, interview (9 May 2001); Syd Shelton and Ruth Gregory, interview (16 May 2001); Red Saunders and Roger Huddle, interview (4 June 2000).
29 Paul T***** interview (24 April 2001).
30 For more on this phenomenon see *Sounds* (25 March 1978), p. 28.
31 Bulldog, 1977–80, *National Front Papers*, Modern Records Centre, University of Warwick, MSS.321.
32 Dave Renton, *When We Touched The Sky*, p. 159.
33 'Skins', *Temporary Hoarding*, No. 6 (Summer 1978).
34 Another writer who resists attempts to separate punk from its fixation on 'profane' symbolism is Michael Bracewell. He discusses this in Michael Bracewell, *England is Mine: Pop life in Albion from Wilde to Goldie* (Flamingo, London, 1998), pp. 36–38.
35 John Rees, interview (13 December 2000).
36 Sabin, *Punk Rock: So What?*, pp. 213–215; Home, *Cranked Up Really High*; Home, *We Mean It Man*.
37 Nicky Tesco, interview (5 December 2000); Bradley, *Bass Culture*, p. 449.
38 Dick Hebdige, *Cut 'n' Mix: Culture, identity and Caribbean music* (Routledge, London, 1990), pp. 90–95; Hebdige, *Subculture*, pp. 54–59, Bradley, *Bass Culture*, ch 11.
39 Paul T***** interview (24 April 2001).
40 Timothy S. Brown's survey of so-called 'Nazi Rock' describes the emergence of the skinhead subculture from the earlier 'Mods'. Although elements in the late 1970s skinhead revival sometimes tried to shed their earlier association with black music, by promoting the harder sound of 'Oi', this was by

no means acceptable to the majority of 'skins', as is indicated by their attendance at ska gigs: Timothy S. Brown, 'Subcultures, Pop Music and Politics: Skinheads and "Nazi rock" in England and Germany', *Journal of Social History*, 38:1 (Fall 2004), www.history.neu.edu/faculty/timothy_ brown/1/documents/Subcultures_Pop_Music_and_Politics.pdf, downloaded 30 January 2008.

41 Gilroy, *There Ain't No Black*, pp. 125–126.

42 Red Saunders and Roger Huddle, interview (4 June 2000); Gilroy, *There Ain't No Black*, p. 120.

43 Bradley, *Bass Culture*, ch 18.

44 Gilroy, *There Ain't No Black*, ch 3. See also: Paul Gilroy, 'Police and Thieves', in Paul Gilroy (ed.), *The Empire Strikes Back: Race and racism in 70s Britain* (Routledge, London, 1992).

45 Cited in Pat Gilbert, *Passion is a Fashion: The real story of the Clash* (Aurum, London, 2005), p. 102.

46 Marcus Grey, *The Clash: Return of the last gang in town* (Helter Skelter, London, 2003), p. 157.

47 Cited in Gilbert, *Passion is a Fashion*, p. 135.

48 Jonathan Coe, *The Rotters' Club* (Penguin, London, 2002), p. 176.

49 The 'hippy' connection is proposed in Sabin, *Punk Rock: So What?*, p. 207.

50 Widgery, *Beating Time*, pp. 85–86; Salewicz, 'Carnival report'.

51 For a discussion of the cultural and political relevance of carnival to immigrants from the Caribbean see: Geraldine Connor and Max Farrar, 'Carnival in Leeds and London, UK: Making new black British subjectivities' in Milla Cozart Riggio (ed.), *Carnival: Culture in Action – The Trinidad Experience* (Routledge, London, 2004).

52 We might also speculate on the similarities between these political struggles of the late twentieth century and the attempts to regulate social life in the early capitalist period in Europe, when carnivalesque celebrations by the lower orders were perceived as a threat to the imposition of bourgeois 'normality'. See Peter Stallybrass and Allon White, 'Bourgeois hysteria and the carnivalesque', in Simon During (ed.), *The Cultural Studies Reader* (Routledge, London, 1999 edition).

53 Cited in C.W. Watson, *Multiculturalism* (Open University Press, Buckingham, 2000), p. 54.

54 Colin Fancy, interview (2 April 2001).

55 Ibid.

56 Ibid.

57 Syd Shelton and Ruth Gregory, interview (16 May 2001).

5

Rock Against Racism, culture and social struggle

Many of those active in socialist circles during the 1960s and early 1970s confirm the suspicion with which 'Americanised' pop music used to be regarded. When the left attempted to give its politics artistic expression it was often through forms that had been filtered through the sieves of Eastern Bloc socialist realism or 'traditional' folk music – what Red Saunders has lampooned as 'Hungarian linocuts' and the 'woolly jumper'.[1] In this chapter I examine some of the political and cultural reasons for this state of affairs and the nature of RAR's reaction against it. One of my aims is to investigate the assumptions of commentators like Dave Laing and Jon Savage, who see in RAR the product of an unsophisticated Marxist approach to cultural matters. In pursuit of this end I compare RAR and the so-called second folk revival, which was arguably the most significant post-war cultural movement on the British left. The revival is particularly important in this context, since it is so closely connected with the British CP and the party's fellow travellers, and as such it represents a useful point of comparison between the cultural activities of different wings of the socialist movement. I have also tried to situate RAR against the background of the 'cultural Marxism' which emerged as a component of the New Left in the 1950s and 1960s and to explain the extent to which a growing concern with forms of cultural critique influenced the activists who founded RAR. This is by no means an exhaustive survey, but it serves as a challenge to some of the more simplistic assertions regarding RAR's aesthetic and political foundations.

RAR occupies a place within a long history of left-wing engagement with culture that has encompassed both artistic production and theoretical appreciation. I have tried to illuminate various strands of RAR's activities, with particular reference to the organisation's analysis of 'post-electronic' popular music and the theoretical assumptions that underlay this. In comparing RAR's project and that undertaken by the artists and theorists who pioneered the post-war folk revival and those who rose to prominence through the New Left, I attempt to cast some light on the cultural politics of Stalinism and of alternative socialist traditions. I have also considered how RAR related to revolutionary currents in the visual arts.

One of the issues with which RAR, the folk revivalists, and the New Left were concerned was the possibility of developing a radical cultural perspective under capitalist conditions, and this entailed defining how the left ought to relate to popular culture. This issue presents the left with a quandary, for modern popular culture is, after all, essentially concerned with the production, sale and consumption of cultural commodities. But for Marxists commodities are powerful and troubling things. They are fetish objects *par excellence*, which embody the exploitative economic relations that lie at the heart of capitalism. As I argued in chapter three, commodities – products of past labour – come to dominate the lives of the very people who produce them, but they also stand in our minds as symbols, potent manifestations of our fears and desires. The source of this peculiar power lies in the commodity's status as the product of a double estrangement. The first estrangement occurs as a precondition of the capitalist mode of production, when workers, lacking any access otherwise to the means of production, are compelled to turn their own labour power into a commodity and to sell it to the bourgeoisie, who in their turn determine the ends to which it will be put. The second estrangement takes place as the products of workers' labour are taken from them and sold in the market place, where, if they encounter them again, it is not as creators but as mere consumers. As Marx puts it in *Capital*:

> The mysterious character of the commodity-form consists therefore simply in the fact that the commodity reflects the social characteristics of men's own labour as objective characteristics of the products of labour themselves, as the socio-natural properties of these things. Hence it also reflects the social relation of the producers to the sum total of labour as a social relation between objects, a relation which exists apart from and outside the producers. Through this substitution, the products of labour become commodities, sensuous things which are at the same time supra-sensible or social.[2]

The profound consequences of this process of alienation and fetishisation are made clear by Marx in the following passage:

> It is nothing but the definite social relation between men themselves which assumes here, for them, the fantastic form of a relation between things. In order, therefore, to find an analogy we must take flight into the misty realm of religion. There the products of the human brain appear as

autonomous figures endowed with a life of their own, which enter into relations both with each other and with the human race. So it is in the world of commodities with the products of men's hands.[3]

Colin Barker's succinct formulation sums this up well: 'In producing commodities, we produce not only useful things, but also a distinct form of society founded on alienated social relations.'[4]

The ubiquity of the commodity and its intrusion into every sphere of our lives, even the most intimate, provides, according to Marxists, the material basis for the most totalising ideological system in all of human history. How, then, can the products of what Adorno and Horkheimer call the 'culture industry' be mobilised in support of a project aimed at consciousness-raising and critical practice? Given the all-pervasive (and invasive) nature of bourgeois ideology – its ability to insinuate itself into the deepest recesses of our psychology and social relations – is it really possible for the left to counter its influence using weapons borrowed from the enemy? Is it the case that under such conditions man will be able, as Marx suggests, to 'face with sober senses, his real conditions of life, and his relations with his kind'?[5]

In this chapter I will be discussing how RAR responded to the challenges outlined above and will look at some of the political and social influences on the organisation's politics. I argue that RAR's approach entailed a rejection both of the Communist Party's Cold War-inflected point of view and of those theorists who despaired of any attempt to break the grip of bourgeois ideology on the working class.

Communists, folk music and working-class culture

The folk music revival that took place in Britain in the aftermath of World War Two continued a process of retrieval and re-presentation of folk cultures that had begun much earlier with the work of researchers like Cecil Sharp and Maud and Helen Karpeles. These Edwardian enthusiasts for 'traditional' British culture shared a conviction that the songs and dances they were documenting and performing were important elements in a national heritage under threat from the forces of modernity and from rival nationalisms. The composer Ralph Vaughan Williams, who was himself deeply influenced by British folk music, remarked that: 'The art of music . . . is the expression of the soul of a nation, and by a nation I mean . . . any community of people who are spiritually bound together by language, environment, history and common ideals, and above all, a continuity with the past.'[6] Cecil Sharp, as Michael Brocken points out, was no less keen than Williams to promote the unique genius of the British nation, and he was sufficiently attuned to the great power rivalries of the early twentieth century to wish to disengage 'Englishness' from any Teutonic connections.[7] Of course any project aimed at establishing the validity of some hermetic British 'tradition' is problematic in the extreme, and as Dave Harker declares: 'What Sharp and his coadjutors did was impose on to the living culture of English working people (few of whom were agricultural labourers), in some parts of some predominantly rural counties in the south-west, notions of history and of culture which owe more to romance than to reality.'[8]

Just as their Edwardian forebears were keen to distinguish 'native' British folk culture from that of powerful continental competitors such as Germany, a similar concern was evident in the post-war folk revival; in the latter case, however, it took shape under very different conditions. This revival reflected the insecurities of an imperial power facing a period of serious decline in status, and its eclipse by the rising might of the USA.

One thing that distinguished post-war revivalism from its earlier incarnation was its determinedly class-conscious ethos. Whereas Sharp, for instance, was keen to promote the virtues of a mythic English national character, a younger generation of folk musicians and researchers, such as A.L. Lloyd, Ewan MacColl and Peggy Seeger, were determined to redefine the folk idiom as one born of class struggle.[9] They came to agree that folk music needed to be appreciated and performed within constraints imposed by various local 'identities', but they were also in the business of rescuing from obscurity some of those cultural achievements of working people that were otherwise left, quite literally, unsung. One of the key institutions in the folk revival was the Workers' Music Association (WMA), which was established in 1936 to provide cultural support to the labour movement. The Communist Party was influential within the WMA and party members took seriously their mission to use music as a means to cultivate more combative and 'progressive' attitudes among the British people. It was under the auspices of the WMA that A.L. Lloyd, a noted Communist historian of British folk music, wrote *The Singing Englishman*, which became one of the seminal texts of the new movement.[10] It is clear that Communists played an important role in the folk revival at all levels and that many of the movement's organisational structures were tied, in one way or another, to the CP. This is not to say that the folk revival was simply a Communist front operation, or that it was directed from party headquarters in King Street; as Gerald Porter argues, it was often party organisations and individuals in the provinces that led the way in establishing folk clubs and promoting folk culture through various means.[11] What is evident, however, is that the politics of the post-war folk scene were deeply influenced by a particular variant of Marxism, but one which bore the marks of a complex (and sometimes contradictory) set of political, social and economic influences. If we are to appreciate the nature of the Communist Party's politics during the 1950s, and hence how these affected its views on cultural issues, we need to take account of the organisation's experiences during the Second World War and its immediate aftermath.

Although the CP laid claim to the mantle of Bolshevism, its politics owed a great deal to the opportunism and compromises that characterised Stalinist *realpolitik*. As the Hitler–Stalin Pact crumbled under the impact of the German *blitzkrieg* on the Eastern Front, the Communist Party performed a swift volte-face that led it into extensive collaboration with Britain's wartime regime. Communist militants' enthusiasm for Joint Production Committees, aimed at maximising industrial production, and the Party's willingness to eulogise their old class enemy Winston Churchill, were lucid expressions of a wholeheartedly popular frontist politics that saw the CP transform itself into one of the most enthusiastic defenders of the 'national good'. As Angus Calder notes:

> Yet the C.P. was once again missing its real opportunity to capture the leadership of the Labour movement. Apart from calls for a second front and for freedom for India, its current policy boiled down to unflinching support for Churchill's coalition – indeed, its major surviving grievance seemed to be that it had not been asked to join it.[12]

Such a perspective could not fail to leave its imprint on the post-war politics of a party which had once fancied itself a valuable partner of the British bourgeoisie.[13] But victory over Germany and the demise of this wartime marriage of convenience did not mean that Britain was, in the CP's eyes, free from danger. Another threat loomed in the shape of the United States. Britain had clearly been displaced as the world's premier imperial power, and American economic and military muscle ensured that the centre of gravity in the western world shifted away from Europe and towards the United States. The onset of the Cold War saw Britain taking the place of junior partner *vis-à-vis* the USA, a relationship that locked the country into a strategic alliance established in opposition to Russia and hence against what the CP fancied to be a workers' state. But the new post-war international settlement was only one of the changes that came to occupy the minds of left-wing theorists and activists. Of crucial importance was the economic boom that followed the war and its influence on the lifestyles and ideas of the working class. The initial euphoria that accompanied the election of Clement Atlee's Labour Government in 1945 soon evaporated, paving the way for thirteen years of Tory government, from 1951 to 1964. Some commentators detected within British society a tendency towards the 'bourgeoisification' of workers, as they succumbed to the allure of a new consumer society built on the back of generalised economic prosperity. As Dennis Dworkin puts it: 'At the root of the problem was the post-war reshaping of working-class consciousness and culture, a consequence of full employment, real increases in income, class mobility, and spreading mass culture.'[14] What is more, leading the charge of this new mass culture were the flashy battalions of the American culture industry. It seemed to some on the left that a nakedly consumerist brand of capitalism was active in reworking the political and communal affiliations of the British working class, whilst at the same time promoting the 'Americanisation' of Britain and the world. The extent of the CP's alarm over American influence can be gathered from Sam Aaronovitch's 1951 article 'The American threat to British culture', which appeared in the party's discussion journal *Arena*:

> We can draw three conclusions from this survey.
>   First: we are not dealing with a problem of 'cultural exchange' but with a systematic, well-organized and financed attempt to impose coca-colonization on the British people. We are dealing with 'cultural imperialism'.
>   Second: this problem does not arise because we have a common language with the Americans. They are doing precisely the same to the peoples of Western Europe.
>   Third: such cultural imperialism, the swamping of Britain with American cultural products of the most degraded and reactionary kind, cannot but retard and damage the cultural development of Britain itself.[15]

That these worries also animated the pioneers of the second folk revival is clear from Ewan MacColl's recollection:

> I became concerned . . . that we had a whole generation who were becoming quasi-Americans, and I felt this was absolutely monstrous! I was convinced that we had a music that was just as vigorous as anything that America has produced, and we should be pursuing some kind of national identity, not just becoming an arm of American cultural imperialism.[16]

The Communist Party's official line on culture was not simply imposed on an inert membership, however; it ran counter to a rather more receptive attitude towards 'Americanised' music on the part of those party members and supporters who had been drawn to jazz during the 1930s and 1940s. The Young Communist League established the *Challenge* jazz club following the war and an environment grew up in which communists and others debated the socio-political and aesthetic dimensions of this young art form. In their discussions these enthusiasts attempted to gauge the status of jazz as a 'people's music', the relative importance of race and class in defining the sociological basis of jazz, the virtues of live versus recorded music, and the links between jazz and other art forms such as surrealism.[17] So rather than seeing the CP's official attitude towards 'Americanised' culture as an inevitable consequence of the party's political theory, we need to appreciate how it existed in a state of tension with competing interpretations. It was the party's attempts to orientate itself in a world riven by inter-imperialist rivalries that encouraged it to swing, in the words of one commentator, 'from a broad-minded progressivism to the bigotries of Zhdanovism'.[18] One concern, however, which taxed jazz and folk revivalists alike, and which will be encountered again with RAR, is how to reconcile left-wing politics with cultural forms often encountered chiefly as commodities.

One way of circumventing the increasing commodification of popular culture was to look backwards, to a time when the working class was more obviously active in the production, rather than mere consumption, of its entertainments and cultural life. This was one of the imperatives recognised by post-war enthusiasts for British folk music, who worked hard to recover traditional ballads, work songs and other forms of music and to perform them to contemporary audiences. In doing so the folk revival articulated some of the preoccupations of prominent Communist Party historians, such as E.P. Thompson, John Saville and Christopher Hill, whose painstaking rediscovery and analysis of the cultural achievements of working people was motivated by a desire to establish a more 'democratic' and socially inclusive approach to history. The congruity between the revivalists' intentions and those of the Communist Party's Historians' Group is evident in Dworkin's assertion that 'Marxist historians saw themselves as restoring to the working class and progressive movements their revolutionary past, a heritage suppressed by several centuries of ruling-class obfuscation'.[19] The folk revival was more than an antiquarian exercise, however, for performers like Ewan MacColl were themselves accomplished songwriters and they added to the canon of British folk music with their own compositions. By building a network of clubs, societies and print media through which folk music could be disseminated and discussed, the revival operated on the fringes of the 'commercial' music scene and hence (arguably) was insulated from the effects of the decadent consumerism that 'folkies' so detested. By bringing working people together in this way, the folk revival created spaces within which politics and culture could potentially be brought into creative fusion.

But the revival went beyond the confines of small music venues. MacColl enlisted the support of producer Charles Parker to create a series of radio broadcasts entitled *The Radio Ballads*. In these ground-breaking productions (which had an ironic counterpoint in the loathing, among many folk music enthusiasts, for modern technological innovations such as the electric guitar) MacColl and Parker employed sophisticated production techniques to explore the lives of people ordinarily ignored by the mass media. Rail workers, miners, gypsies and fishermen were among the subjects of these programmes, for which MacColl wrote many new songs. These excursions into radio combined spoken word, sound and music and, uniquely for the time, MacColl and Parker insisted that the interviews they recorded in their travels were not re-voiced using actors.[20] Despite such daring departures, however, it is evident that the folk revival's narrow cultural compass, and the prescriptive aesthetic standards that its leading figures came to impose on performers inhibited whatever potential existed for a genuinely populist appeal to the working class, and especially young workers. Not the least of its problems in this regard was the folk revival's stringent anti-Americanism.

The folk revivalists' attempts to diminish the influence of American popular culture among British workers were in accord with the political priorities established by the Communist Party during the Cold War, but they also slipped easily into a popular-frontist, progressive patriotism to which all classes could subscribe, based upon the identification of a 'British cultural heritage' free from the taint of 'Americanism'.[21] This combination of 'progressive nationalism' and proletarian 'authenticity' was an awkward amalgam, which could lead to remarkably conservative conclusions. The drive to eradicate what some left-wingers saw as decadent cosmopolitan influences within national cultures, for instance, could prompt demands for ethnically defined norms of purity within musical expression. It was a short step from the disavowal of American cultural contamination to an insistence that performers should confine themselves to exploring their 'own' folk traditions. Ewan MacColl thus reacted to the runaway growth of commercial pop music by imposing a 'policy rule' into folk clubs under his influence, which demanded that performers 'should limit themselves to songs which were in a language the singer spoke or understood'.[22] MacColl's willingness, earlier in the decade, to perform black American music alongside like-minded jazz musicians, had become transformed, by the late 1950s, into a dogmatic refusal to tolerate 'a bloke from Walthamstow pretending to be from China or from the Mississippi'.[23] This erosion of the autonomy and interpretive role of the performer was in no way Marxist, but it does recall the Stalinist intolerance of cultural heterodoxy. What is more, the striving for absolute fidelity to a rigidly defined folk archetype led certain purists to discourage any sort of musical accompaniment to singing, let alone the use of electrical instrumentation. The absurdity of this position became clear when black American musicians were invited to tour Britain and had to perform without their electric instruments for fear of offending the revivalists.[24] But perhaps the most famous manifestation of this nostalgic myopia came during Bob Dylan's famous 1966 concert at the Free Trade Hall in Manchester, when a cry of 'Judas' greeted Dylan and his backing band as they performed an electric set. What had begun as a desire to rescue folk traditions from (to borrow E.P. Thompson's phrase) the 'enormous condescension of posterity' had evolved into a movement which celebrated the parochial and the rustic.[25] 'Progressive' nationalism and a kind of romantic technophobia came to characterise much of the music associated with the folk revival, and these sentiments helped to cut the left off from a real appreciation of black American music and thus from the cultural life of growing numbers of British youngsters.

   Although the folk revival shared some of the concerns of figures such as E.P. Thompson, including the commitment 'to the kind of cultural struggle which was felt to be especially urgent in the conditions of "consumer capitalism" ',[26] the section of the movement most closely associated with MacColl came to embody a type of top-down, elitist attitude towards politics and culture that many in the emerging New Left defined themselves against. Whereas Thompson was keen to rescue the history of working people from obscurity in order to reinstate workers as subjects, rather than mere objects, of history, all too often the cultural prejudices of the folk revival contradicted the movement's avowed intentions and instead tended to posit 'working-class culture' as a set of static practices and attitudes, to be policed by the guardians of 'authenticity'. However, at a time when folk revivalists were trying to stem the tide of commercialism and Americanisation within popular culture, the New Left had embarked on a project that would lead some influential intellectuals towards a view of popular culture as a contradictory, and potentially subversive, phenomenon. Rather than simply lamenting the loss of proletarian traditions, and decrying the passivity of consumer society, these theorists and activists turned an analytical spotlight on the contexts within which consumption was occurring and the manifold ways in which consumers were actively fashioning new identities and modes of life from the materials furnished by capitalism.[27] We need to strike a note of caution here, for the New Left did not speak with a single voice, and some of its conclusions were decidedly pessimistic. Richard Hoggart's description of milk bar culture in the 1950s, for example, would not have seemed out of place in the pages of *Arena*:

> Compared even with the pub around the corner, this is all a peculiarly thin and pallid form of dissipation, a sort of spiritual dry-rot amid the odour of boiled milk. Many of the customers – their clothes, their hair-styles, their facial expressions all indicate – are living to a large extent in a myth-world compounded of a few simple elements which they take to be those of American life.[28]

Despite such sceptical broadsides, however, it remains the case that the rise of the New Left afforded an opportunity for socialists to reconsider their attitudes towards popular culture. Following the precedent set by the pioneering work of dissident CP historians, important sections of the left began to develop an approach to cultural politics that eschewed the folk revival's blanket refusal to engage with forms of music that were enjoyed by the broad masses. It is this tendency, rather than that represented by the folk revivalists, which seems truer to Thompson's declaration that class formation is 'an active process, which owes as much to agency as conditioning'.[29] It is noteworthy, too, that the anti-populist sentiments of some critics of 'mass culture' were being aired at a time when British popular culture was showing signs of renewed vitality. Commenting on playwright Arnold Wesker's concerns regarding the spread of 'cultural mediocrity', David Watt declares:

> The accusation of a 'cultural snobbery' which assumed that 'popular equals bad' levelled at Wesker in particular was indicative of a substantial cultural blind spot (far from peculiar to Wesker at the time) just at the moment when the emergence of the Beatles was unsettling the dominance of American popular culture and opening up possibilities of a different sort of indigenous, hands-on music-making, and the emergence on television of a grainy working-class realism represented by the popularity of *Z-Cars*, the one-off plays of David Mercer and others, and the documentary work of Denis Mitchell, Ken Loach, and others indicated a radical potential in the 'popular' media.[30]

Setting the context for RAR: the New Left and the rise of British cultural Marxism

The political ideas that animated RAR need to be set in a very different context to those that inspired the post-war folk revival. Britain in 1976 faced social and economic conditions which bore little resemblance to those that obtained after the war, and the left itself was far more fragmented both organisationally and ideologically. Of particular note, the two decades between the watershed year of 1956 and the founding of RAR witnessed the emergence of new political movements that had shed the left's traditional preoccupation with class struggle in favour of an emphasis on cultural critique and identity politics. It is significant, however, that although the SWP had been influenced by this trend, it never yielded its emphasis on class, and this continued allegiance to 'classical Marxism' had a direct influence on RAR's attitude towards culture.

By 1976 the British left had experienced several decades of dramatic change, including the schism that had opened up within communist ranks following the Russian invasion of Hungary in 1956. Combined with the revelations in Nikita Khrushchev's speech to the twentieth congress of the Communist Party of the Soviet Union in February of that year, in which the Russian leader denounced the crimes of Stalin and attacked the 'cult of the personality', this act of imperialist aggression prompted many communists to question their commitment to a movement which supported the crushing of workers' councils in Budapest in the name of 'freedom and independence'.[31] The growth of a New Left, centred initially on dissident Communist historians like E.P. Thompson and John Saville, signalled the start of protracted attempts to fashion a viable socialist politics that drew inspiration from Marx, but which broke sharply with the rigid dogmas of Stalinist orthodoxy.

Practically from its first stirrings, however, the New Left incorporated two poles of attraction that – although linked – pulled in different directions. One section of the New Left coalesced around Thompson and Saville, and it found its voice through the journal *The Reasoner* (later *The New Reasoner*), which was an internal party publication aimed at fellow 'loyal communists'. This tendency was still attached to principles of organisation and theory that were recognisably Marxian and as such it sought to draw recruits from the CP and the wider labour movement (most notably the left wing of the Labour Party), and it aimed to establish a mass base through involvement in popular protests such as the Campaign for Nuclear Disarmament. The most important expression of the new movement's politics was the 'socialist humanism' explicated by Thompson, which sought to replace the crude determinism of Stalinism with a politics that restored the human subject to the central role in history that Marx originally envisaged.

But the Stalinist forgets that the 'economic base' is a fiction descriptive not of men's physical-economic activities alone, but of their moral and intellectual being as well. Production, distribution and consumption are not only digging, carrying and eating, but are also planning, organising and enjoying. Imaginative and intellectual faculties are not confined to a 'superstructure' and erected upon a 'base' of things (including menthings); they are implicit in the creative act of labour which makes man man.[32]

This 'socialism from below' was most clearly elucidated through the writings of Thompson and Saville, and fellow historians such as Eric Hobsbawm, George Rudé and Christopher Hill, all of whom produced innovative studies that reaffirmed the creative contributions of 'ordinary' people to historical events.

But besides these fugitives from the CP, a second New Left began to take shape, away from the environs of the labour movement and within the less tradition-bound precincts of academia. Speaking mainly through the journal *Universities & Left Review*, this section of the movement began to develop a 'socio-cultural', rather than a straightforwardly 'political', response to the crisis within socialism.[33] Although obviously influenced by events in eastern Europe, the proponents of what Peter Sedgwick dubbed 'Socio-Culture' strove to describe and explain the ways in which post-war prosperity and the rise of consumer society were reshaping the lives of the masses under capitalism. Their chief objects of study became 'the cultural mass media and their effects on popular moral and social consciousness'.[34] Richard Hoggart's *The Uses of Literacy* and Raymond Williams's *Culture and Society* and *The Long Revolution* became canonical texts, and younger theorists like Stuart Hall began to shape the debate over culture and class with articles suggesting that Marxists needed to modify their views on class formation to take more account of the impact of consumerism.

> Whilst it may have been true, in the past, as Raymond Williams argues, that 'the working class does not become bourgeois by owning the new products', that working class culture is a 'whole way of life' not reducible to its artefacts, it may now be less and less true, because the 'new things' *in themselves* suggest and imply a way of life which has become objectified *through them*, and may even become desirable because of their social value.[35]

And later:

> The break-up of a 'whole way of life' into a series of life-styles (so-called 'lower-middle class' unfolding into 'middle-middle class', and so on, upwards) means that life is now a series of fragmented patterns for living for many working class people. One cannot organise militantly to keep up with the Joneses. Moreover, many must feel a personal repugnance against involving themselves with a series of interlocking rat-races. But what else can they do? Self-improvement and self-advancement are now

parts of the same process. That is the message of the capitalism of the proletariat. That is the tragic conflict within a working class which has freed itself only for new and more subtle forms of enslavement.[36]

Although a formal unity between the 'political' and 'socio-cultural' wings of the New Left was enacted when the *New Reasoner* and *Universities & Left Review* merged to become the *New Left Review* in 1960, it was the latter tendency that became hegemonic. As time passed the movement fragmented, with many of its most prominent spokespeople, such as Stuart Hall, establishing a strong presence in academia as researchers and theorists.

The burgeoning field of cultural studies grew largely from seeds sown in the New Left and one of its most important institutional settings was the Centre for Contemporary Cultural Studies established at the University of Birmingham. Initially under the directorship of Richard Hoggart, the Centre undertook extensive research into popular and youth culture and so began to reset the parameters of cultural appreciation to include many of those forms, such as rock and jazz music, popular cinema, and youth subcultures, which the earlier folk purists and the CP derided as commercially debased 'Americana'.[37] This newfound regard for the products of popular culture coincided with the interests of people like David Widgery, Red Saunders and Roger Huddle, who despaired of the traditional left's unwillingness to embrace the everyday realities of modern, cosmopolitan, urban life. But unlike their counterparts in the New Left, Widgery and his comrades were unwilling to surrender their allegiance to a Marxist project that maintained its focus on class struggle. Although RAR was dedicated to forms of activity and organisation that in some ways challenged long-established traditions and habits on the left, many of the key figures who founded the movement stayed loyal to their overarching commitment to the labour movement and revolutionary socialism. The reasons for this lie in the nature of the crisis that initially precipitated the formation of the New Left and the political perspectives that distinguished the International Socialist tendency from the Communist Party.

The New Left's preoccupation with re-establishing the centrality of the human subject in politics and history is well documented. The historiography of E.P. Thompson and the popular-cultural investigations of Stuart Hall both attest to the New Left's willingness to look beneath surface appearances, to the social and ideological forces that – often in obscurity – shape our history. But as we have seen, Tony Cliff had proposed a similar reorientation on the human subject, but from a perspective deeply rooted in the class politics of revolutionaries like Marx,

Engels, Luxemburg, Lenin and Trotsky. That Cliff was determined to reaffirm the role of human agency in shaping the world is clear from his claim that: 'Crucially, the theory of state capitalism put the concept of the emancipation of the workers as the act of the working class itself back at the centre of Marxism'.[38] When Khrushchev delivered his condemnation of Stalin and Russian tanks rolled into Budapest, many communists received this as a traumatic shock; what they had hitherto regarded as Marxist orthodoxy stood revealed as a counter-revolutionary justification for oppression and exploitation. In their haste to discard the ideological trappings of Stalinism, many of those communists who abandoned the CP also cut their ties to elements of the Marxist tradition, such as Bolshevism and the centrality of the working class, which they felt had been fatally compromised by their association with Stalin's Russia. It was scarcely surprising, then, that the splits and tensions caused by the events of 1956 – combined with a lengthy economic boom that seemed to confirm the essential vigour of capitalism – should prompt so many socialists to gravitate towards new forms of radical activity within fields such as cultural criticism and identity politics. For Cliff and his small group of fellow thinkers, however, no such fundamental realignment was implied by the revelation that Stalinism was a corrupt and reactionary social and ideological force. Rather, from the point of view of the IS, 1956 vindicated their theoretical viewpoint, which was founded upon an attempt to revive the very 'classical Marxist' tradition that so many socialists were now abandoning.

What is more, where the socio-cultural theorists of the New Left saw a British working class lulled into apathy through the allure of plentiful consumer goods and a tendency among workers to define themselves through consumption rather than production, Cliff took a different view. He proposed that the favourable economic climate produced by the post-war boom made it possible for workers to extract concessions from employers without recourse to national bargaining and the formal apparatus of the traditional labour movement. This 'reformism from below' was not an abandonment of class struggle, but rather 'its diversion into different channels'.[39] As long as the influence of shop stewards and small-scale industrial action could achieve real gains, political activities such as parliamentary lobbying and manoeuvring between trade union bureaucrats and MPs seemed of little relevance to many workers. Cliff's perspective still held out the prospect of a resurgence in class struggle when economic conditions undercut the profits that made grassroots reformism viable, but more importantly in the context of this discussion, the SWP's position denied that socialists needed to abandon fundamental elements of their politics in light of the rise of 'consumer society'. To effectively relate to workers Marxists did not need to rethink their ideas about class in order to agitate around a multiplicity of new culturally constructed identities, and nor was it appropriate to indulge in abstruse cultural critique; rather, revolutionaries needed to formulate political and organisational responses to a class struggle that manifested itself in many different ways, but which was still essentially rooted in the exploitative relationship between capital and labour. Although some SWP activists came to believe that the left as a whole was insufficiently sensitive to the potential for cultural politics, they still accepted that this needed to be set within the context of a political movement aimed at the revolutionary overthrow of capitalism, and that the dominant antagonism within this struggle was to do with class rather than identity. This orientation is expressed clearly by Chris Harman, writing in 1979:

> In a downturn in the class struggle, it is the duty of revolutionary organi-
> sations to relate to all sorts of movements that develop outside the work-
> places among oppressed and exploited groups. But, it has to do this while
> never forgetting that the agent of revolutionary change lies elsewhere.
> 'Where the chains of capitalism are forged, there they must be smashed'.
> And the link with the working class movement has to be an active one,
> not merely a rhetorical one. The revolutionary organisation has to search
> out and connect with the smallest spark of working class resistance against
> the system, even in a period in which its own growth comes mainly from
> the 'marginal' areas. Otherwise it will not be able to relate to the agent
> of revolutionary change when it begins to stir.[40]

RAR: culture and social struggle

RAR's embrace of electric rock music signalled the organisation's determination to challenge the insularity and elitism of much of the left. As former *Socialist Worker* journalist Laurie Flynn put it:

> The closet intellectuals who lead London's revolutionary groups view
> themselves as highly sophisticated people but they are in reality superbly
> parochial. They think only about class, not about consciousness. They
> don't seem to understand that any meaningful socialism has culture not
> only at its core, but *as* its core. They are philistine about many things,
> none more so than music, having no conception of its position in the
> consciousness industries of our time. Almost without exception, they
> refuse the novelty, the richness, the idiosyncrasy of their own experience,
> the sixties, preferring ancient algebras to serious reflection and trouble-
> some thoughts.[41]

Those socialists within the SWP who were impatient with the culturally timid politics lambasted by Flynn were aided in their goal of relating to trends in modern music by a political orientation which distanced them from the left's generalised animosity towards the USA. This attitude opened up a space within which some of them could develop a fruitful engagement with American popular culture. Even if, by the 1970s, some of the heat had been taken out of the Communist Party's fierce condemnation of the USA's influence in cultural matters, anti-American attitudes resurfaced in the Stalinised politics of various 'Third-worldist' and Maoist groups, whose emphasis on anti-colonial struggles led them to place an enormous emphasis on combating US cultural imperialism. On the Trotskyist left, too, anti-Americanism flowed from the politics of those 'orthodox' tendencies which insisted that Russia and similar societies represented degenerated or deformed workers' states that needed shielding from American capitalism.

Of immense importance to RAR was the experience, shared by many of the movement's enthusiasts, of participating in counter-cultural politics in the 1960s. This was a formative influence on Red Saunders, whose political awareness was heightened through his visceral sense of injustice, rather than a close scrutiny of Lenin's writings, and he and Roger Huddle recount how, for them, the great social struggles of the 1960s were enmeshed in, and mediated through, their growing love for popular music.[42] This experience allowed RAR to propose ways of engaging with young people that drew on these connections.

It is important to grasp at this point the link between artistic vitality and social conflict that animated RAR's founders and which informed their view of the modernist tradition to which they felt an allegiance. It is not the case that RAR's identity was simply derived from particular youth subcultures – most obviously punk rock and reggae – it also drew on influences from other sources. In a 2007 radio interview, when discussing RAR's graphic style, Red Saunders cited the following inspirations: 'Soviet constructivism and American pop art, linked in with European modernism.'[43] RAR's concern, however, was not simply to revive certain styles, but to establish a productive relationship between political and cultural activities. As Roger Huddle explains, 'the major thing about modernity in the twentieth century was, when it was linked to a social struggle, it did its best work.'[44] This point is relevant in two ways. Firstly, the artistic products of previous high points in struggle are, in themselves, valuable assets. In establishing this bond with the past, Saunders and Huddle were continuing a process of retrieval and re-presentation we have already seen at work in the post-war folk revival and the historiography of New Left historians. Secondly, Huddle is claiming that artists do not operate simply as individuals, but rather their work is informed and enriched through their connection to wider social forces. As a case in point, the Soviet constructivism to which

Saunders refers marked a point where the social dynamism and optimism of the October Revolution was still sufficient to inspire advances
in avant-garde art. Furthermore, Huddle makes clear that this understanding of radical culture is embedded in his political education within
the SWP, which stressed the creative role of the rank and file worker
alongside the necessity of 'professional' organisation.[45]

Huddle's remarks on the dynamics of cultural activism are clearly
informed by Marx's analysis of ideology; an analysis which stresses the
links between the different dimensions of human experience. For Marx,
ideology cannot be understood simply as a set of more or less coherent
ideas that gain sway through their persuasiveness or logical consistency.
Rather, ideology articulates a lived relationship with the world around
us, a relationship which is at once personal and social and which can
be summed up in Marx's observation that 'Man is a ζῶον πολιτικόν
[*zoon politikon* – social animal] in the most literal sense: he is not only
a social animal, but an animal that can individualise himself only within
society.'[46] The intimacy of the link between the individual human being
and his or her social surroundings is what gives rise to Marx's famous
declaration that 'It is not the consciousness of men that determines their
being, but, on the contrary, their social being that determines their
consciousness.'[47] This passage is often paraphrased as 'being determines
consciousness', but such a construction transforms a statement which
sheds light on one of the cornerstones of Marxism – the human condi-
tion as an essentially social experience – into a much more abstract
declaration, which can be read as a vague existentialist maxim. Marx's
assertion of the primacy of 'social being' over 'consciousness' is, after
all, not merely a philosophical conjecture but a call to arms. He demands
a practical engagement with the world, rather than a merely contempla-
tive or moralistic attitude towards it. For Marx and his followers the
key to changing the ideas in people's minds lies in transforming the
ways in which they relate to society. As Marx puts it in his *Theses
on Feuerbach*, this is a question of promoting ' "practical-critical"
[i.e. revolutionary], activity'.[48]

In light of these considerations it should be apparent that a Marxist
approach to anti-racism should not be confined simply to didactic
methods and goals; breaking the grip of racism on people's minds
cannot be achieved merely through an appeal to reason, or through
mobilising sophisticated arguments. As important as theoretical clarity
undoubtedly is in the Marxist project, unless political ideas are put at
the service of workers in struggle, they will tend to be both ineffective
and beyond the reach of practical critique. This latter point is crucial,
for Marxists believe it is only through testing ideas in the arena of

political and social struggle that one can gauge their validity and effectiveness. What matters most in mounting a challenge to the bourgeoisie's cultural and ideological hegemony is not the internal consistency of one's vision, but rather its ability to provide a critique of existing social relations that can be translated into meaningful action. Ideas need to build a bond between revolutionaries and those layers in society who are beginning to move towards opposition, they need to cement a working alliance, not simply provide a kind of ideological accompaniment to mutual laments about the injustices of capitalism.

Given the considerations outlined above, we can understand the urgency with which RAR sought to find a practical basis for its anti-racist work; this led the organisation to reject a number of elitist assumptions which had characterised some attempts on the left to marry culture and politics. So, rather than reinventing and disseminating a supposedly authentic working-class culture, or bemoaning workers' failure to appreciate bourgeois high art, RAR hoped to make an *active* connection with young people through the medium of their *existing* enthusiasms. In this way, RAR attempted to avoid the narrowly didactic attitude of Music For Socialism (MFS), which was set up at around the same time as RAR, but which operated on the basis 'that the music itself must first be political'. One MFS theorist even admitted that they 'tended to produce music (traditional folk, free jazz) which most people could not understand or enjoy'.[49] While this approach may have provided an aesthetic balm for those who disapproved of the unsophisticated tastes of the working class, it provided MFS with only the most tenuous claim on the attentions of black and white British youth. Furthermore, those socialists who supported the organisation were faced with the implausible task of dictating the tastes of a generation of music fans and, in the process, weaning them off the products of the commercial music industry.

Marx's notion, that 'social being determines consciousness', provides a clue to understanding RAR's permissive attitude towards highly commercialised popular music. Prominent figures in RAR, such as Huddle and Widgery, rejected the assumption that workers are passive consumers of ideologically loaded cultural products, insisting instead that the ways in which culture is experienced contribute to its effect. Rather than positing the audience as a torpid, undiscriminating mass, RAR strove to provide a forum within which young people could do more than merely consume cultural commodities. This explains RAR's refusal to demand political conformity from the musical acts that it staged, or to turn away swastika-wearing punks from gigs. The important thing to grasp, it is claimed, is the context in which the music was performed and heard, and the clothes worn. Colin Fancy explains that the music at RAR gigs was often apolitical, but it would be performed in front of a RAR backdrop, anti-racist stickers and badges would be sported, *Temporary Hoarding* was on sale and political debate was rife: 'Anyone who . . . did get hung up on what the band were saying, it felt wrong, because it was much more important what the audience was saying and thinking . . . was the audience prepared to listen to black and white music together?'[50] A RAR organiser in Leeds declared: 'You know what makes it worthwhile? When a kid comes up to you and tells you he used to go to Front meetings and they [sic] way they treated him compared to the way Rock Against Racism treats him (friendly like) has made him think twice.'[51]

This perspective, in which the audience participates actively in the reception of culture and is potentially transformed as a result, is prefigured in Brecht's use of montage techniques in his theatrical productions. In constantly challenging the audience's assumptions and prejudices, Brecht invites them to adopt a critical attitude towards the work presented to them. In her study of the writer and critic Walter Benjamin, Esther Leslie comments on Benjamin's appreciation of Brecht's theatre in terms which could also apply to RAR:

> [H]e is concerned with patterns of reception, the 'relations of production' that artworks imply. The artist is a producer but not a proletarian. Benjamin reformulates the problematic in terms of the animated category of agency and not the dormant sociologistic statement of class. But, in effect, it is not only the artist who is a producer, but also the viewer, the consumer of culture. A stance that considers the mode of reception as central to the question of the political nature of art contrasts with those theses on committed art that assume reception is not a theoretical issue and, consequently, that the factors, 'political commitment', technique and literary 'quality' have no dialectical relationship to one another.[52]

The humanist Marxism of the SWP provided a congenial environment in which cultural activists could start to reassess the left's generally negative attitude towards popular culture. The central role of human agency in history, which Cliff reiterated, and which featured so strongly both in Marx's writings on ideology and in much of British post-war cultural Marxism, allowed scope for a more optimistic appreciation of the consumer's place in the culture industry than many on the left were willing to countenance. What also seems apparent, however, is that RAR provided an opportunity for the SWP to remain politically active (even if this was in what Chris Harman deemed a 'marginal' area), and so maintain the party's connections with 'oppressed and exploited groups' during a period marked by a serious decline in the militancy of the industrial working class.

It is notable that the attitudes of some RAR activists echo Leon Trotsky's writings on art and culture. One of Trotsky's aims in the post-revolutionary period in Russia was to counter the arguments of certain artists who were impatiently demanding the promulgation of a truly proletarian culture, even as the material resources of the new soviet republic were being stretched to breaking point. Far from aiming appeals above the heads of the working class, as the advocates of so-called 'Proletkult' were wont to do, Trotsky recognised the necessity of a lengthy period of cultural and moral development on the part of the proletariat, even following its seizure of state power. Such a delicate and inherently unpredictable process could not be circumvented through merely bureaucratic manoeuvres, or the substitution of the will of a cultured minority for the consciousness of the masses. Proletkult's demand for the creation of specifically proletarian forms of culture could, perhaps, be attributed to an excess of revolutionary zeal, but the increasing bureaucratisation of Russian society presented an increasingly powerful threat to artistic freedom, and Trotsky did not shrink from warning the Communist Party against interfering heavy-handedly in artistic affairs.

Although Trotsky regarded art as an important component of a post-capitalist society and one of the ways in which the alienation of workers from their creative capacities could be overcome, he argued that talk of establishing a truly proletarian culture was not merely premature, but implausible. Since workers' power demands from the outset the expropriation of its oppressors' property, it cannot follow the bourgeoisie's example and develop as a cultural and economic power within the interstices of the social order it seeks to overthrow. And if Marx is right, and the death of capitalism ushers in the eradication of all class divisions, then the working class succeeds in establishing a fully communist society only insofar as it removes the material basis for its own existence as a distinct stratum of society. As Trotsky puts it when discussing the prospects for cultural development during the transition to socialism:

> The cultural reconstruction which will begin when the need of the iron clutch of a dictatorship unparalleled in history will have disappeared will not have a class character. This seems to lead to the conclusion that there is no proletarian culture and that there never will be any and in fact there is no reason to regret this. The proletariat acquires power for the purpose of doing away forever with class culture and to make way for human culture. We frequently seem to forget this.[53]

Although they were separated from Trotsky's experiences by several decades, during which the cultural lives of the world's working classes had been radically transformed, it is possible to discern in the attitudes of RAR's founders and supporters something of the same anti-elitist spirit. This much is evident in the SWP's lack of a prescriptive line on art, which, in any case, was low on the list of priorities for a small dissident group, aiming to establish itself as a presence within the industrial working class.[54] SWP activists may have participated in the British folk scene, which was a feature of the left during the 1960s, but this seems to have been motivated by personal tastes, rather than any deep ideological conviction regarding the political efficacy of folk music.[55] SWP member Ian Birchall revealed a more open-minded view of electric pop music than was typical on the on the left, when he declared: 'What does concern me, however, is the contemptuous attitude to so-called "pop music" by so many people on the Left. Partly this contempt seems to spring from a belief that any form of art that has an enormous popularity must be necessarily inferior – a curiously elitist position for socialists.'[56] This recalls Trotsky's criticism of Russian Futurists, amongst others, for failing to take existing conditions as the starting point for their art.[57] It also cuts against the pessimistic view that workers had become so mesmerised by the material and ideological products of capitalism that they were incapable of envisioning, let alone building, a better society.[58]

As I intimated earlier, if we are to make sense of RAR's politico-cultural trajectory we need to be sensitive not only to the theoretical basis of the movement's politics, but also the personal experiences of many of its key activists and supporters. Lots of these veterans of industrial and political struggles were able to transfer their skills in building rank and file and united front organisations to the task of connecting with broad masses of young working class people. The links between political mobilisation and popular culture had already been explored at length by a number of RAR's leading figures, as a glance at their CVs indicates. David Widgery was well known within the cultural avant-garde that grew up around *Oz* magazine and he was active in major protest movements such as the campaign against the Vietnam War.[59] Red Saunders, the man who instigated RAR, was an ex-mod and close to the SWP; as a member of CAST (Cartoon Archetypal Slogan Theatre), he accompanied SWP national speaking tours, writing and performing plays that accompanied the political speeches and rallies.[60] Roger Huddle ran a mobile disco, 'Night Train', and joined with Sheila Rowbotham (whom he knew through the Labour Party Young Socialists and IS) in criticising the formulaic doctrines of much of the left.[61] The unique circumstances of the 1960s thus introduced the SWP to a generation of radicals shaped by a combination of counter-culture, 'agit-prop', pop music and humanist Marxism.

The potential for instigating a counter-cultural movement along the lines of RAR was heightened by the influx into socialist ranks of intellectuals and campaigners from the student protests of the 1960s. These recruits accounted for a significant portion of the SWP's growth during the latter part of the decade,[62] and even though many were later marginal to RAR, their sympathies were at least informed by the sensibilities of 1960s cultural and political radicalism.[63] The SWP could not be described as a hotbed of hippy idealism, but it appealed to some of those young people for whom socialism and culture were equally passionate commitments. David Widgery even claimed he was prompted to join the organisation on the strength of an obituary of André Breton written by Ian Birchall.[64]

Modernism old and new

I have already suggested that RAR deliberately employed modernist modes of expression often associated with the Russian revolutionary experience, but it is also significant that the design methodology of RAR coincided at certain points with the bricolage style of punk rock. The aesthetics of surrealism, so beloved of David Widgery, have an obvious affinity with the punk practice of creating bizarre juxtapositions and shocking contrasts.[65] Fashion ensembles of bin bags and fishnet stockings betray a strong family resemblance to RAR montages, such as the row of sieg-heiling Nazis with RAR yo-yos dangling from their outstretched hands.[66] This common ground is one of the reasons why RAR's founders understood that punks who carelessly incorporated fascist symbols into their wardrobe were not necessarily endorsing the far-right's politics. Modernism's embrace of ambiguity and 'self-reflexiveness', and its association with creative techniques such as photo-montage, provided the cultural enthusiasts who pioneered RAR with a set of precedents and models that could help them negotiate the aesthetic landscape of punk.

Given the breadth of RAR's cultural influences it is clear that the movement did more than simply appropriate punk's stylistic conventions. *Temporary Hoarding* is a case in point. Several commentators claim that the RAR journal simply aped the style and format of amateur fanzines, and indeed there is an undeniable influence in terms of typography, imagery and layout. However, the magazine's designers reject the charge of plagiarism. Syd Shelton and Ruth Gregory make it clear that, although they were inspired by some punk graphics, they were most interested in developing aesthetic practices that reflected modern developments in printing and reproduction technology. In Shelton's words, 'technological change had a lot to do with inspiring us to use new . . . ways of producing . . . getting images on pages'.[67] The spread of offset lithography in newspaper production was prominent among these changes, but the advent of cheap photocopying, new darkroom techniques and graphics products such as *Letraset* all played a part. The design professionals who worked for RAR were far removed from the enthusiastic amateurs who put together A4 fanzines at home: as Syd Shelton puts it: 'This is not trying to copy fanzines, I assure you . . . we were in a different category than sticking it together in your bedroom.'[68] Shelton's and Gregory's concern with marrying technology and aesthetics bears a direct relationship with those Russian revolutionary artists whom Red Saunders cited as a key influence on RAR's graphic style.

The degree to which *Temporary Hoarding*'s design advanced its mission to communicate politics to a youthful audience is open to debate. The paper undoubtedly represented a striking alternative to the traditionally mundane style of left-wing publications and Paul Gilroy gave it an enthusiastic endorsement, but RAR activist Colin Fancy thought that *Temporary Hoarding*'s graphics, with the exception of some of the montage posters, might have got in the way of the readership. The precedent he felt was most clearly evident in *Temporary Hoarding* was the underground press of the 1960s and early 1970s. Besides, as an avid reader of music papers and fanzines, Fancy was impatient with the lengthy discussions and opinion pieces that appeared in *Temporary Hoarding*. As he recounts: 'I looked at these articles today . . . about internment or about feminism, whatever, they passed me by, they completely passed me by. I don't know what *Temporary Hoarding*'s audience was, but, y'know, I was a music press and fanzine reader and I wanted to read interviews with bands.'[69]

Such an interpretation is rejected by David Widgery, who emphasises *Temporary Hoarding*'s role as a vital organising tool, which had proved its popularity by achieving a circulation of 12,000 by 1979.[70]

What the debate over *Temporary Hoarding* helps to illuminate is the active role taken by RAR as a cultural force in its own right. This was part and parcel of RAR's innovative approach to a perplexing problem on the left: how can socialists appeal to the aesthetic sensibilities of a mass audience when these are dominated by the products of an unashamedly commercialised culture industry? The political movers behind the folk revival assumed that the musicians themselves had to exemplify certain ideals in terms of musical production and performance. In response to misgivings about the Americanisation of British culture and the alienation of workers from the means of cultural production, communists and their fellow travellers attempted to carve out a niche within which relatively pure forms of folk music could be created and appreciated. If this simultaneously cut the movement off from a mass audience, then this connection would presumably have to be rebuilt through a lengthy process of education. In this situation the organising bodies of the folk revival acted as political sponsors and arbiters of taste, but not directly as a creative force *per se*. In a similar vein, movements such as the Nicaragua Solidarity Campaign deployed musicians as direct representatives of the victims of imperialist aggression: particular forms of national folk music thus became the aesthetic expression of a political campaign which was otherwise carried out through the traditional forms of pamphleteering, socials, street demonstrations and so on. RAR was different. Although punk and reggae certainly fulfilled some of the requirements of authentic 'folk' music, and their ability to perform the role of 'dissident' cultures owed something to their status as voices of rebellion, they were clearly not divorced in any fundamental sense from the commercialism of the music industry. Punk may have embodied a tension between the creative autonomy of the subculture's various participants and the nullifying effects of commercial co-option, but it could not sustain this opposition indefinitely. The idea that punk and reggae represented an alternative to the products of capitalist culture was rather more rhetorical than realistic, but what did score in their favour was that their popularity and accessibility allowed them to act as a pole of attraction for a mass audience, rather than merely an enlightened elite. Despite their accommodation with the commercial machinery of capitalism, however, RAR's leading figures did not abandon the idea that a radical left-wing culture is attainable under such conditions. Their shift in focus away from the stage and towards the audience, though, meant placing less emphasis on the mechanics of music production and more on the context within which music is consumed. RAR, in this sense, was more concerned with identifying music as one constituent of 'social being' than in laying bare the precise character of popular music as a commodity form.

Although music was still the at the core of RAR's appeal to youth, it was presented within a particular context, the defining characteristics of which were shaped by RAR both as an organising body and as a creator of a well-defined cultural identity. Thus the magazines, flyers, badges, journalism, concert backdrops, speeches, carnival spectacles, and so on, all came to embody RAR's message in a far more consistent manner than could be achieved by straightforwardly showcasing the loose coalition of musicians and performers who lent their talents to the campaign. In a sense, RAR's cultural activity was a model for the kind of radical fusion of art and politics to which so many of its founders aspired; an aspiration that was prefigured in the work of artists such as Mayakovsky, Rodchenko, Brecht and Eisenstein.

Summary

RAR's approach to popular culture was influenced by a particular interpretation of modernism, which in turn was shaped by a specific strain of Marxist politics. The SWP's attempt to establish a humanist Marxism in opposition to Stalinist orthodoxy was achieved through an act of reclamation: the 'classical Marxism' that Tony Cliff claimed had been distorted and obscured by decades of misrepresentation was instead harnessed to a political project aimed at restoring to socialism the centrality of human agency and class struggle. Faced with the reality of America's post-war economic, political and military hegemony in the West, and the onset of a period of dynamic growth for global capitalism, the SWP felt the need neither to emulate the Cold War-influenced attitudes of much of the British left, nor to search for 'socio-cultural' alternatives to Marxism's traditional emphasis on class as the primary division within capitalist society. Under the influence of the SWP's politics, RAR was able to develop an unusually positive (for the British left) appreciation of 'Americanised' youth culture. RAR's attempt to link political and cultural activism was, at least in part, aimed at creating the conditions in which a critical culture could thrive and in this sense the most important thing was not so much the explicit politics of particular artists as the context in which they operated. The stage may have provided the theatrical focus for RAR events, but the organisers were concerned mainly with the role of the audience. This orientation offered a way of escaping the fixed dualism of producer and consumer, through positing both as active participants in a broader process of political engagement and cultural production.

The modernist tradition to which RAR appealed was used both as a template from which to generate a strong visual identity and as an example of the potency of cultural activity when aligned with popular radicalism. The degree to which RAR succeeded in fusing its political and cultural aims is debatable – some would argue, for instance, that the organisation's sophisticated grasp of the significance of fascist symbolism within punk rock was not matched by its apparent naivety regarding the mobilisation of the red star as its own logo. It seems widely accepted, however, that RAR's innovative use of graphics and imagery was, on the whole, a success and RAR's designers make it clear that this was due to more than a keen eye for punk-inspired trends in design. It is also the case that RAR embodied a dual status, as an organising/political body, and as a cultural producer. To this extent RAR followed in the footsteps of the second folk revival, although the focus in RAR's case was in recontextualising particular forms of music and performance, rather than in creating the music itself.

Notes

1 Red Saunders and Roger Huddle, interview (4 June 2000); Widgery, *Beating Time*, p. 56.
2 Karl Marx, *Capital: Volume 1* (Penguin, Middlesex, 1976), pp. 164–165.
3 Marx, *Capital: Volume 1*, p. 165.
4 Colin Barker, 'A "new" reformism?', *International Socialism Journal*, 2:4 (Spring 1979), p. 89.
5 Karl Marx and Frederick Engels, 'Manifesto of the Communist Party', in Karl Marx and Frederick Engels, *Selected Works in One Volume* (Lawrence and Wishart, London, 1968), p. 38.
6 Cited in: Brocken, *The British Folk Revival*, p. 8 (ellipsis in Brocken).
7 Brocken, *The British Folk Revival*, p. 8.
8 Harker, *One For The Money*, p. 147.
9 Denselow, *When The Music's Over*, pp. 22–23.
10 Brocken, *The British Folk Revival*, pp. 49–51.
11 Gerald Porter, '"The World's Ill-Divided"', pp. 171–172.
12 Angus Calder, *The People's War: Britain 1939–1945* (Pimlico, London, 1992), p. 348.
13 The enthusiasm with which the CP supported the wartime coalition (not to mention General Secretary Harry Pollitt's close friendly relations with the newspaper magnate Lord Beaverbrook) is clear in: Francis Beckett, *Enemy Within: The rise and fall of the British Communist Party* (Merlin, London, 1995), pp. 98–100. A revealing contemporary appeal to national unity, from a prominent CP member is: R. Palme Dutt, *Britain in the World Front* (Lawrence & Wishart, London, 1942).
14 Dennis Dworkin, *Cultural Marxism in Postwar Britain: History, the New Left and cultural studies* (Duke University Press, London, 1997), p. 57.
15 Sam Aaronovitch, 'The American threat to British culture', *Arena*, 2:8 (June/July 1951), p. 13. This issue was given over to the proceedings of the Communist Party's 1951 conference, also called 'The American Threat to British Culture'.
16 Denselow, *When The Music's Over*, p. 26.
17 Kevin Morgan, 'King Street blues: jazz and the left in Britain in the 1930s–1940s', in Croft, *Weapon in the Struggle*. The Communist Party historian Eric Hobsbawm was perhaps the CP's most prominent jazz enthusiast, a subject he wrote about under the pseudonym Francis Newton.

18 Morgan, 'King Street blues', p. 124. The word 'Zhdanovism' denotes the kind of authoritarian demands typical of Stalin's chief spokesman on artistic questions, Andrei Zhdanov. For more on this see: Maynard Solomon, *Marxism and Art* (Harvester Press, Brighton, 1979), pp. 235–241.

19 Dworkin, *Cultural Marxism*, p. 38.

20 Denselow, *When The Music's Over*, pp. 23–26.

21 Aaronovitch, 'The American threat'; Diana Sinnot, 'Our historical tradition', *Arena*, 2:8 (June/July 1951), pp. 23–24.

22 Ewan MacColl, *Journeyman: An autobiography* (Sidgwick & Jackson, London, 1990), pp. 287–278.

23 Denselow, *When The Music's Over*, pp. 23–26.

24 Wally Whyton's reminiscence is cited in: Dr Mike Brocken, *The British Folk Revival*, PhD Thesis, http://web.ukonline.co.uk/mustrad/articles/broc-ndx. htm, downloaded 30 July 2001.

25 The aversion of many left-wing 'folkies' to technological innovation is noteworthy. It is interesting to consider why so many Communists, who were willing to engage in rampant technophilia when it came to lauding Russian achievements in industry, should succumb to its opposite in cultural matters. This may be partly due to the CP's popular frontism. In honouring its commitment to compromise with the bourgeoisie it will have been helpful for the CP to look backwards to a working class located in a safely distant and heavily mythologised past, rather than forwards, to the revolutionary overthrow of capitalism. But Communists' unease with American technological advances may also express a degree of insecurity in the face of western capitalism's post-war boom. One of the ideas underpinning some, but not all, strands of Marxism is that the working class will seize control of the productive forces generated under capitalism and develop them to a higher level than the bourgeoisie could hope to attain. The Eastern Bloc economies hardly presented such a prospect in the post-war period, so Stalinist parties may have felt more comfortable in promoting Communism as the bearer of the best moral qualities of the working class, rather than a powerful spur to material advance.

26 Ellen Meiksins Wood, 'A chronology of the New Left and its successors, or: who's old-fashioned now?', http://socialistregister.com, downloaded 9 May 2007.

27 Dworkin, *Cultural Marxism*, pp. 4–5.

28 Richard Hoggart, *The Uses of Literacy* (Penguin books in association with Chatto & Windus, Harmondsworth, 1958), p. 248.

29 E.P. Thompson, *The Making of the English Working Class* (Penguin, London, 1991), p. 8.

30 David Watt, 'The maker and the tool': Charles Parker, documentary performance and the search for a popular culture, *New Theatre Quarterly*, 73:9, Part 1 (February 2003).

31 The phrase is taken from a radio broadcast by Janos Kadar, the man who led the attack on the Hungarian revolution and who later became the country's leader. From: Chris Harman, *Class Struggles in Eastern Europe*

1945–83 (London, Bookmarks, 1988), p. 140. See also: Bideleux and Jeffries, *A History of Eastern Europe*, p. 532.

32 E.P. Thompson, 'Socialist humanism: an epistle to the Philistines', *The New Reasoner*, 1 (Summer 1957), p. 131.

33 Peter Sedgwick, 'The two New Lefts', *International Socialism Journal*, 1:17 (August 1964), reprinted in David Widgery, *The Left in Britain 1956–1968* (London, Penguin, 1976), ch 3.

34 Peter Sedgwick, 'The two New Lefts', p. 137.

35 Stuart Hall, 'A Sense of classlessness', *Universities & Left Review*, No. 5 (Autumn 1958), p. 29 (emphasis in original).

36 Stuart Hall, 'A Sense of classlessness', p. 31.

37 For a good overview of the development of cultural studies in Britain see: Dworkin, *Cultural Marxism*, ch 3.

38 Tony Cliff, *A World To Win*, p. 44.

39 Callinicos, *Trotskyism*, pp. 84–85. See also Paul Blackledge, 'The New Left's renewal of Marxism', *International Socialism Journal*, 2:112 (Autumn 2006).

40 Chris Harman, 'The crisis of the European revolutionary left', *International Socialism Journal*, 2:4 (Spring 1979), p. 84.

41 Widgery, *Beating Time*, pp. 83–84.

42 Red Saunders and Roger Huddle, interview (4 June 2000).

43 *Rockin' Against Racism*, BBC Radio 4 (26 June 2007).

44 Red Saunders and Roger Huddle, interview (4 June 2000).

45 Ibid.

46 Karl Marx, 'Introduction to a critique of political economy', supplementary text to *The German Ideology: Part One* (Lawrence & Wishart, London, 1970), p. 125.

47 Karl Marx, 'Preface to a contribution to the critique of political economy', Marx and Engels, *Selected Works*, p. 181.

48 Karl Marx, 'Theses on Feuerbach', Marx and Engels, *Selected Works*, p. 28.

49 J. Hoyland and M. Flood-Page, 'You can lead a horse to water', *Socialist Review* (June 1978), p. 17; Huddle, 'Hard Rain'.

50 Colin Fancy, interview (2 April 2001).

51 *Temporary Hoarding*, No. 7 (Winter 1979), p. 11.

52 Esther Leslie, *Walter Benjamin: Overpowering conformism* (Pluto, London, 2000), p. 99.

53 Leon Trotsky, *Literature and Revolution*, pp. 214–215.

54 Tony Cliff, for one, maintained scant interest in cultural matters in later life, see Tony Cliff, 'Influences', *New Statesman* (16 September 1994), p. 13.

55 Ian Birchall, personal communication (2 September 2001).

56 Ian Birchall, 'Don't knock pop music', *Young Guard* (June 1964), p. 7. See also: 'Culture', *Young Guard* (September 1963), p. 6; 'Pop music dialectics', *Young Guard* (April 1965), p. 5.

57 Leon Trotsky, *Literature and Revolution*, p. 168.

58 Theodor Adorno and Max Horkheimer, *The Culture Industry: Enlighten-ment as mass deception*, www.marxists.org/reference/archive/adorno/1944/culture-industry.htm, downloaded 20 November 2007; Leszek Kolakowski, *Main Currents of Marxism* (Oxford University Press, Oxford, 1981), vol. 3, ch X; Joanne Hollows, 'Mass culture theory and political economy', in Joanne Hollows and Mark Jancovich (eds), *Approaches to Popular Film* (Manchester University Press, Manchester, 1995).

59 Renton, *The Poetics of Propaganda*.

60 Red Saunders and Roger Huddle, interview (4 June 2000).

61 Ibid.; Huddle, 'Hard Rain', pp. 12–13. Sheila Rowbotham's memoir of her experiences in the 1960s captures some of the politico-cultural turmoil that pre-dated RAR: Sheila Rowbotham, *Promise of a Dream: Remember-ing the sixties* (Penguin, London, 2000).

62 Ian Birchall, *Mass Party*.

63 David Widgery, *The Left in Britain*, chs 7 and 8.

64 David Widgery, 'Agitprop and the SWP', *Wedge*, No. 2 (Spring 1978), pp. 44–45, *Alistair Mutch Papers*, Modern Records Centre, University of Warwick, MSS.284.

65 See Hebdige, *Subculture*, pp. 102–106. The link with the situationist practice of *détournement* is also apparent; see *Détournement as Negation and Prelude*, http://library.nothingness.org/articles/SI/en/display/315, downloaded 20 November 2007.

66 *Temporary Hoarding*, No. 11 (January/February 1980).

67 Syd Shelton and Ruth Gregory, interview (16 May 2001).

68 Ibid.

69 Colin Fancy, interview (2 April 2001).

70 Widgery, *Beating Time*, p. 62.

6

Aftermath

Over a quarter of a century has passed since RAR staged its final concert, and it would be implausible within the constraints of this study to consider all of the trends and movements that have attempted to unite popular music and politics since that time.[1] It is possible, nonetheless, to assess the extent to which some of these projects have been informed by RAR's style of culturally engaged agit-prop. Although a relatively modest undertaking, such an exercise will enable us to illuminate a number of the political and cultural assumptions underlying these other campaigns and it will also help us judge the applicability of the 'RAR model' to movements created in circumstances far removed from those that attended the birth of the anti-racist struggle in 1970s Britain. With these ends in mind I will focus on two initiatives which exemplify – at least in their explicit intentions – contrasting attitudes towards the cultural politics of RAR. These are Love Music Hate Racism (LMHR), and the series of appeals, led by Bob Geldof, to combat famine and poverty in Africa.

Love Music Hate Racism was founded in 2002 in response to the electoral threat from an increasingly confident British National Party (BNP) and a perceived rise in the level of racist attacks in Britain. The organisation, which borrows its name from an old RAR slogan, has positioned itself as a direct heir to Rock Against Racism and shares a number of the older campaign's political affiliations. Geldof's interventions, on the other hand, starting with the Band Aid single 'Do They Know It's Christmas?' and the 1985 Live Aid concerts, and concluding with the Live 8 concerts staged in 2005 during the Gleneagles G8 summit, represent an approach to pop and politics that is, in important ways, directly at odds with the RAR model. Before considering specific events, however, it is important to appreciate some of the ways in which popular music has altered since the early 1980s. I wish to examine in particular some of the recent social and technological influences on pop music's ethnic boundaries. The examples I cite will necessarily be rather

selective, but hopefully they exemplify tendencies that can be generalised more widely.

By the time RAR staged its final carnival in Leeds in 1981, the politico-cultural terrain upon which the movement operated had changed
considerably. The rising fortunes of the Conservative Party under Margaret Thatcher, culminating in their general election victory in 1979,
and the simultaneous descent of the NF into terminal splits and political
irrelevance, heralded enormous changes on the right of British politics.
But although the threat from fascism had been confronted and deci-
sively beaten, Thatcherism posed new problems for the left to surmount.
On the culture front, RAR's success in fostering a self-consciously tolerant and diverse popular-cultural milieu could be judged by the presence
at the Leeds carnival of the Specials, a multi-racial band signed to the
Two-Tone record label, and one of a number of groups, such as the Beat
and UB40, whose black and white band members played music inspired
directly by Caribbean styles such as ska and reggae. The cross-cultural
fusion that had been such a strong feature of RAR gigs, and which was
deeply marked by its debt to Jamaican-inspired musical forms, had
become generalised to the extent that, as David Widgery put it in 1986:
'Racially and sexually mixed bands, from Working Week to Culture
Club are now two a penny.'[2]

In the period since the Leeds carnival the tendency for popular music
to absorb influences from diverse ethnic and cultural origins has grown
in strength. One person who has come to appreciate this development
is Nicky Tesco, who, when interviewed in 2000, suggested that any
attempt to reinvent RAR would need to come to terms with the fact
that contemporary dance music provides a far more cosmopolitan
and accessible platform than the partnership between punk and reggae
fostered in the 1970s[3] – an observation borne out by the emergence
of large numbers of performers whose music incorporates influences
from around the world. Bhangra, for instance, a form of music and
dance with its origins in rural Punjab, but which has been preserved
among Britain's Indian communities, has mutated and found its way
into the repertoires of contemporary British and American artists and
producers. Southall-born producer Rishi Rich has been at the forefront
of this development, and his collaborators have included not only UK
rappers and DJs, but international stars with high media profiles,
such as Craig David and Ricky Martin. The complex interplay between
Asian modes of expression and other forms of music has meanwhile
been explored by artists like Fun-Da-Mental and Asian Dub Foundation
– performers and writers whose sharp polemical edge and political
commitment draw strength from these connections. In France, meanwhile, Algerian 'rai', has reached beyond France's large north African

population to mix with styles such as hip-hop and punk, to produce dance music that draws on complex middle-eastern rhythms and the life experiences of immigrant workers. The prominence of rap music in this context – derived from African-American precedents, but remixed and relocated in a Franco-African setting – confirms the flexibility of a genre that can transfer its deep attachment to the spoken word to any linguistic community. It could also be argued that the French state's attempts to defend its 'native' recording industry and performers has aided the development of a thriving musical culture among the country's Francophone immigrant population. Legislation demanding that 40 per cent of the songs played on French radio should be in sung in French may not have radically revived the fortunes of the traditional 'chanson française', but it did stimulate demand for domestic rap music, and it created a market for artists who might otherwise have found their voices muted by the preponderance of Anglo-American product.[4]

It is clear from the examples of bhangra and rai that, in Britain and France at least, a history of imperial expansion and contraction in Africa and Asia has helped to form the channels along which cultural transfers flow. But emigrants do not necessarily follow a path from colonial 'periphery' to metropolitan 'centre'. Capitalism's global ambitions demand a degree of labour mobility that encourages a constant intermingling of peoples and cultures, as do the frequent crises and wars that produce sudden increases in the numbers of refugees and asylum seekers. Both processes are evident in the continual flow of people across the USA's borders, and which has contributed to all forms of American popular culture.[5] In *City of Quartz*, Mike Davis's dazzling study of Los Angeles, he speculates on the cultural possibilities of a city struggling to accommodate multiple economic, social and cultural influences, and in doing so he suggests the kinds of tensions that are becoming increasingly apparent in cities across the globe:

> In this emerging, poly-ethnic and poly-lingual society – with Anglos a declining minority – the structural conditions of intervention in popular culture are constantly in flux. Who can predict how the long years of struggle which lie ahead, before new Latino immigrants can hope to attain social and political equality, will affect the culture of the Spanish-speaking inner city? Will the city-within-the-city become colonized by a neo-Taiwanese work ethic of thrift and submission, disintegrate into a clock-work-orange of warring gangs, produce an oppositional subculture (like the Yiddish radicalism of ragtime New York) – or, perhaps, all three? Equally, will the boundaries between different groups become faultlines of conflict or high-voltage generators of an alternative urban culture led by poly-ethnic vanguards?[6]

The effects of social conflict on the production and reception of popular music can be seen in the work of artists whose music has come to symbolise resistance to oppression, and in the responses to it of individuals and groups who sympathise with the struggles and concerns that these artists represent. The anti-apartheid movement, to give one example, provided a forum within which African and 'western' musicians could cooperate in registering their opposition to racism, and audiences could participate in a celebration of the vitality and creativity of 'subaltern' cultures. Resistance to apartheid, within and beyond South Africa, encouraged the kind of cross-cultural solidarity that helped to generate an international audience for acts like Ladysmith Black Mambazo, and Mahlathini and the Mahotella Queens, who performed music derived from styles popular in South African townships.[7] Meanwhile, eminent exiles from apartheid, such as jazz trumpeter Hugh Masekela and singer Miriam Makeba, built successful careers in Europe and America, often playing at anti-apartheid events alongside sympathetic performers from around the world.[8]

Besides the constant ebb and flow of populations, and the influence exercised by individual artists, the technologies through which music is produced and distributed have transformed both the conditions under which popular music has developed since the 1970s and the range of cultural actors involved in this process. One aspect of the changes wrought by new technologies is the way cheap and portable recording media have extended the reach of the music industry. This is especially so as the successors to vinyl have opened up the possibilities of home recording and the production of personalised playlists. Commenting on the potential for cassette tapes to reach hitherto untapped audiences, Simon Frith asserted, 'any music may now be heard any time anywhere',[9] but the subsequent spread of accessible forms of digital manipulation, recording and transfer, have extended even further our access to an enormously broad range of music whilst simultaneously putting within easy reach the means to originate, sample and disseminate it. Combined with internet-based resources such as file-sharing websites, and online sales and marketing, the borders between nationally specific cultures have become far more permeable; a process accelerated by the growth of multinational media networks built around powerful and pervasive means of communication like satellite TV and the World Wide Web. The cross-cultural implications of these globally extended conglomerations of technology and capital have been drawn out by Rehan Hyder:

Apart from financial benefits and associated economies of scale, co-operation between major and independent labels has another significant

effect, that which accords localized music access to global flows of communication. By using the international communication networks set up to
serve the global markets, of which the music industry is but one, individuals and groups can facilitate the processes of cultural syncretism and
exchange on a global scale. These international networks, as well as
enabling major corporations to maximize their profits and the flow of
international capital have become proactive in the development of new
dynamic musical forms and the emergence of new syncretic manifestations
of cultural identity.[10]

But the ease with which modern technologies facilitate the amalgama-
tion of disparate cultural influences is not synonymous with the democ-
ratisation of musical production. There is a tension here, between the
potential for grassroots innovation that is opened up by new technologies and the ability of capitalism to co-opt and suborn cultures that may
appear initially as counter-hegemonic. Naomi Klein has described how
sportswear giants like Nike and Adidas have allied themselves with
gangster rappers in pursuit of the inner-city black dollar,[11] and John
Hutnyk has criticised the romanticised consumption of 'cultural "difference"' at events staged by Womad (World Music and Dance). Hutnyk
observes that: 'Laments for a pre-industrial music manifest in many
ways, not least of all in the rhetoric of Womad, even at the very moment
when it is the technological extension of market economies that is the
ground of possibility upon which it is staged.'[12] There are widespread
reservations about artists who attempt to 'spice up' their acts by incorpo-
rating elements derived from 'third world' contexts. The fact that, in
many cases, this involves appropriating musical forms and modes of performance from nations that were once imperial possessions or dependen-
cies of the great powers, brings to the fore the complicated power-relations
implicit in such transactions.[13] A tendency to essentialise dynamic and
fluid cultural practices, and to 'fix' them as easily assimilable chunks
represents, for some observers, the operation of a kind of 'tourist gaze',
that fixes the 'other' within a framework that perpetuates particular relations of domination and submission. But the tendency of capitalism to
commodify and reify the 'hybrid' cultures that result from its technologi-
cally enhanced intrusion into every aspect of global cultural production
is not entirely negative, for commodities themselves are not simply
bearers of the disabling ideology of consumerism. Commodities both
embody the exploitative social relations of capitalism and symbolise the
thwarted ambitions of the consumer. Accordingly, acts of consumption
are never entirely free of contradiction, for there is always a utopian
element present in our relationship with commodities. In her comments
on Walter Benjamin's *Arcades Project*, Esther Leslie makes this point:

'At the same time as consciousness is colonised by the commodity, consciousness responds to the utopian side of commodity production, holding open a space for genuine response to the presentations of commodified desires. The impulse for accepting the commodity is the actual wish to see dreams fulfilled.'[14] At the heart of commodity fetishism is an insoluble contradiction: the hopes and desires we hope to satisfy through consuming commodities will never be sated through the fetishistic appropriation of these objects of desire. As much as it tries to divert social and individual discontents into the well-worn ruts of consumerism, the curse of commodity fetishism is to provoke and evoke appetites that capitalism is incapable of satisfying. Indeed, capital accumulation relies upon this restless interplay between innovation and dissatisfaction.

I wish neither to uncritically foreground the liberating potential of new technologies that allow us to sample and mix diverse musical forms, nor to condemn as simply reactionary these same practices. I would, rather, draw attention to the contradictoriness of activities that at once combine and hybridise cultures, but do so on terms mediated via processes of exploitation and oppression and the various forms of *resistance* that these provoke. For it is not enough simply to draw attention to the reifying effects of popular culture; one also has to appreciate – as did RAR – that pop culture does not merely disseminate and reproduce the dominant ideas within capitalism, but also represents a potential site of struggle. We have seen how this bore fruit in the anti-racist mobilisations of the 1970s, but even where youth subcultures are doing their 'traditional' job of articulating inter-generational strife, they can corrode habits of deference across a broad front: it is notable, for instance, that the appeal of rai and bhangra is frequently most keenly felt among urban youth – often second-generation immigrants – who are eager not only to contest their subordinate status within the 'host' society, but also to signal their alienation from 'traditional' customs and values, including those relating to dress, alcohol and sexuality.[15]

Bob Geldof and the 'Aid' projects

If the cultural basis of popular music has expanded since 1981, it has also maintained its capacity to act as a rallying point for various social issues. The scope and scale of the relationship between political and social causes on the one hand, and what Reebee Garofalo characterises as 'mass music' on the other, is evident from a brief survey of the issues addressed through protest music: these include racism, apartheid, the plight of poor American farmers, drug abuse, women's oppression, gay rights, Thatcherism, the Falklands War, the war in Iraq and nuclear disarmament. Undoubtedly the most significant such politico-cultural initiative of the last thirty years, however, has been the campaign, led by Bob Geldof, against famine and poverty in Africa. First the release of the Band Aid single in 1984, then the Live Aid concerts in London and Philadelphia in 1985, saw Geldof champion a brand of politics which shared at least some of the distinguishing features of Rock Against Racism. Like RAR, Band Aid and Live Aid focused on a particular issue – raising funds to help alleviate the effects of famine in Ethiopia – although, unlike RAR, the campaign's approach to this central issue was not embedded in a broader left-wing political project. Geldof's later involvement in the protests around the Gleneagles G8 summit in 2005 entailed a change in emphasis from famine to poverty and debt relief, and this immediately put under scrutiny those powerful states and financial institutions that Geldof believed should be pressurised into solving the problem of global poverty. His decision to stage the Live 8 concerts, and his determination to ally himself with a movement with explicitly political, rather than simply humanitarian, ends, seemed to evoke even more clearly than his earlier efforts the principles of a movement dedicated to combining the pleasures of popular music with the principles of mass action.

David Widgery for one, recognised the affinities with RAR when he wrote of Band Aid, 'like RAR, it is a practical response to a crisis conventional politics clearly can't handle'. And later, commenting on the 1985 concerts staged in London and Philadelphia, 'the rock and roll spirit of getting on and *doing* something, the audacious internationalism of the TV transmission and the way [the] electronic audience could for once feel part of a culture that could act collectively, were all exhilarating'.[16] The enormous scale of Geldof's enterprise is evident in the estimated £150 million raised through these concerts and the global audience of around 1.5 billion that watched the Live Aid events.[17] Geldof's considerably enhanced status as an authority on African affairs, and the degree to which world leaders took seriously the need to at least appear sympathetic to his cause, gave birth to what became known as 'punk diplomacy'. As John Street, Seth Hague and Heather Savigny note, however, Geldof did not understand 'punk' as 'some collectively generated chaos, but rather as individualist, anti-institutional politics; the ability and opportunity to speak out freely, uninhibited by convention or dogma (as he saw them)'.[18]

Although Widgery appreciated Live Aid's audacity and inventiveness, he raised criticisms of a sort that have frequently been aired regarding the political and cultural assumptions underlying Geldof's ventures. Firstly, he admonishes Geldof's 'refusal to find a space for black British bands who have contributed so much to the culture and had organised the first benefit for food to Ethiopia ten years earlier with a bill that included Bob Marley and the Wailers'.[19] Widgery then takes Geldof to task in the following terms, regarding his relationship with the 'establishment':

> The political problem was not that Live Aid failed to overthrow imperialism, East and West (which it never intended) but it became so obsessed with Access card numbers it neglected its other declared intention, to really hammer the big powers' refusal of effective aid. Geldof was not '*too egotistic*', rather he was too easily steered from confronting Thatcher to having off-the-record dinner with the royals, partly because it was too much a one-man band.[20]

The twenty years separating Live Aid from its later incarnation as Live 8 saw major changes in the social and political contexts within which the events took place. In 1984–85, Bob Geldof was raising the profile of an issue – famine relief – that may have been a core concern of charities such as Oxfam, but had not engaged the active sympathies of the popular masses in the developed world. To this extent Live Aid was filling a vacuum. In contrast to this, the 2005 protests around the Gleneagles G8 summit took place only a few years after the groundbreaking demonstrations against the World Trade Organisation meeting in Seattle in 1999, which inaugurated a global anti-capitalist movement with widespread grassroots support and political ambitions that extended far beyond charitable fund-raising. In 1984–85 Geldof found himself, by default, leading a campaign, but in 2005 he and fellow musician Bono were racing to place themselves at the head of an already established movement, and one which had displayed considerable levels of militancy and radicalism. Despite the 1985 and 2005 concerts taking place against such different backdrops, they were, nonetheless, motivated by strikingly similar sentiments. In particular, and despite Geldof's apparent iconoclasm, Live Aid and Live 8 offered no explicit challenge to the power structures from which they hoped to wrest concessions. In this context it is worthwhile comparing Widgery's remarks cited above, with those of George Monbiot, who in the run-up to the protests against the 2005 G8 summit, discussed the attitude of Geldof and Bono to the rich and powerful figures with whom they were dealing:

> I understand the game they're playing. They believe that praising the world's most powerful men is more persuasive than criticising them. The problem is that in doing so they turn the political campaign developed by

the global justice movement into a philanthropic one. They urge the G8 leaders to do more to help the poor. But they say nothing about ceasing to do harm.

I have yet to read a statement by either rock star that suggests a critique of power. They appear to believe that a consensus can be achieved between the powerful and the powerless, that they can assemble a great global chorus of rich and poor to sing from the same sheet. They do not seem to understand that, while the G8 maintains its grip on the instruments of global governance, a shared anthem of peace and love is about as meaningful as the old Coca-Cola ad.[21]

For his part, Geldof has long insisted that the aims of the movement against poverty and famine can be achieved only through negotiating with the handful of powerful political actors who dominate global economics and politics. Explaining his views in a *Guardian* article, Geldof writes: 'you must engage with the process as it is. Not as you imagine it to be, or as you would wish it to be, or even as you think it should be – but as it is. You must engage with the power and the persons and institutions and methods that wield that power.'[22] The many millions of people who responded to the message of Band Aid and Live Aid were therefore useful to the cause in two main ways: as donors of money, and as a source of legitimacy for the figureheads of the movement.[23] Geldof's aim has never been to facilitate the development of a 'counter-public' that could directly challenge the economic and political priorities that generate poverty and famine, but rather to mobilise large numbers of people in order to dramatise and legitimise the actions of himself and other prominent spokespeople for the anti-poverty movement. This offers a sharp contrast with RAR's model of 'bottom-up' activism, and in the context of the struggle against the economic and social priorities of neo-liberalism, Geldof's deliberately 'substitutionist' posture ignores the kinds of radical alternatives being explored in places like Bolivia, where mass protests toppled a government and eventually led to the nationalisation of the country's oil and gas reserves.[24] Furthermore, the Make Poverty History campaign, under whose auspices Live 8 was organised, made clear its intention to limit the terms of the debate over global poverty by refusing to allow groups to affiliate – such as the Stop the War Coalition – which wanted to claim a link between imperialism and social injustice.[25]

The largely passive role that Live Aid and Live 8 assigned to their supporters can be detected not only in the overt politics of these events, but in the cultural 'policy' they shared. As I have noted above, in 1985 Geldof found himself confronting criticisms of his attitude towards black musicians. The 1985 London concert was notable for its lack of black artists, as was the Live 8 London event. Geldof's justification for this is that he is colour-blind when it comes to selecting acts to perform at these shows, and that the artists he wants to encourage are those that have the greatest appeal to a global television audience. Writing in his autobiography, Geldof recounts an argument with a black music journalist where he declares: 'There aren't any world-famous million-selling reggae bands. If Bob Marley were alive I'd be on my knees begging him to play, but no one's heard of Aswad outside the universities. Put them on the telly and people will switch off.'[26] At the end of 2005 the argument is identical: 'To get to the greatest number of people around the world, we had to use the biggest selling artists in the world, nationally and internationally. For all their great musicianship, African acts do not sell many records. People wouldn't watch. Networks wouldn't take the concert.'[27] Street et al observe that such statements, although they appear to be merely pragmatic and factual:

> disguise a political judgement, one which promotes a particular populist vision. It shapes the form of participation just as surely as do the processes that organise and legitimate the participation. Live8 created a movement that was located close to the centre of the contemporary society and politics, a version of Royal Ascot or Wimbledon for popular politics. RAR stood on the fringes, contained in a counter-public sphere. Both linked music to political participation, but in doing so gave life to very different values and experiences.[28]

Although Geldof was able to shrug off critics in 1985, the incongruity between the ostensibly global appeal of Live 8 and Geldof's insistence on marginalising African musicians saw other Live 8 luminaries such as Peter Gabriel insist on an African presence as part of the main Live 8 events. In the end, however, Gabriel and Senegalese musician Youssou N'Dour had to content themselves with co-hosting a separate 'Africa Calling' concert at the Eden project in Cornwall.

In part, of course, the distinctions between RAR and Live Aid can be explained by their different intentions. RAR was explicitly aimed at building a 'movement', rooted in the self-activity of its network of affiliated groups and supporters, but Live Aid and Live 8 were one-off campaigning initiatives. These differences in aims and objectives are not simply tactical choices, however: they are founded upon radically different conceptions of political activity and the nature of power under capitalism. In their analysis of Bob Geldof's role in the Live Aid and Live 8 campaigns, John Street, Seth Hague and Heather Savigny draw attention to the fact that, for Geldof, the political efficacy of popular music has nothing to do with its ability to articulate particular ideas or feelings, or its connection to critical subcultural tendencies. Rather, music is of use only insofar as it can attract a mass audience and hence generate large amounts of revenue. Where RAR embodied an approach to cultural politics that attempted to nurture the critical tendencies within subcultures such as punk and reggae, Live Aid and Live 8 employed music for its populist appeal, rather than its counter-cultural potential. This articulates a politics that is 'conservative in the sense that it sets out to reflect pre-established tastes, measured by units sold. It is also conservative in confining popular "participation" to texting and watching, and leaving active involvement to the elite. Underneath the logic of its politics is the logic of consumption.'[29]

It would be misleading to claim that Geldof completely eschewed the celebratory and emotionally charged qualities of much popular music, but Live Aid and Live 8 offered cathartic experiences; essentially passive routines of carefully staged protest, consumption and alms-giving that did nothing to challenge the ideological presuppositions of the socio-economic system within which the music industry is embedded. To have created a space within which Live Aid's supporters could freely develop their anger and compassion into a thoroughgoing critique of the social and economic priorities of global capitalism would have required engaging them in the kinds of active participation in the campaign that Geldof always discouraged.

Whereas RAR exploited the political potential of musical forms and subcultures that encapsulated implicitly oppositional themes, Geldof's insistence on securing the support of only the most mainstream artists carried with it a tendency to automatically exclude genuinely challenging alternatives to the bland options served up by the music industry. This difference in emphasis should not blind us to an important parallel between RAR and Live Aid, for both campaigns acknowledged the status of pop music as a commodity. Unlike the folk revival, which strove to carve out a niche beyond the commercial mainstream of popular music, RAR and Live Aid embraced the existing tastes of an established constituency of music consumers. But this shared reluctance to shun the products of the music industry as intrinsically reactionary sits alongside sharp differences between the two campaigns. To sum it up in simple terms: whereas RAR utilised popular music *despite* its commodification, Live Aid embraced only the most *highly commodified* forms of popular music. Where RAR sought to challenge the fetishistic character of popular music, through engaging its supporters in forms of practical activity that loosened the grip of ideology, Live Aid dedicated itself to building a base of concerned, but largely passive donors and supporters. RAR attempted to burrow beneath the glossy exterior of the commodity form, to liberate the utopian potential of the human desires encoded within it, but Live Aid engaged with popular music as pure commodity – as a source of revenue and vicarious glamour. Where Live Aid strove to build the largest possible audience, RAR struggled to engage its audience as activists. The joint RAR/ANL carnivals provided one manifestation of this commitment. What a comparison between RAR and Live Aid demonstrates is a contrast between the reformist insistence on decoupling politics from the everyday lives of working people, and revolutionaries' attempts to re-forge those links at every opportunity.

Love Music Hate Racism

Just as Live 8 in 2005 represented an attempt to apply Bob Geldof's original vision of a mass consciousness-raising event to new conditions, so Love Music Hate Racism embodies a similar attempt to re-imagine RAR's mission for the early twenty-first century. Established in direct opposition to the BNP, LMHR has from the outset explicitly identified itself with RAR's heritage. The organisation's name is derived from one of RAR's original slogans: 'Reggae, Soul, Rock 'n' Roll, Jazz, Funk and Punk, our music. Love music hate racism'. Continuity with RAR is clear in LMHR's practice of using popular music as a weapon in the struggle against racism, the main outlets for which are concerts and carnivals. Also like RAR, LMHR advances explicitly political aims whilst simultaneously exploiting the implicitly multi-racial and multicultural nature of modern music to exemplify its mission. The campaign, like RAR, has strong links with the SWP, with party members being involved both directly, and as activists within allied organisations such as Unite Against Fascism (UAF). But despite the obvious similarities between LMHR and RAR, there are also clear differences. Just as Live 8 represented an adaptation of the original Live Aid concept to a different situation, so LMHR has been established in a set of circumstances that will not permit a simple re-run of earlier experiences of anti-racist activism. Before considering LMHR specifically, however, it is worth considering some of the factors bearing upon political organisations generally and the ways in which these shape the relationships between campaigning bodies and their intended audiences. An appreciation of these influences will help to consolidate our understanding of the differences between distinct modes of organisation, and it will also allow us to consider more carefully the ways in which particular political principles can take different forms according to the circumstances in which they are implemented.

Any movement that seeks to sustain the active engagement of its supporters beyond episodic acts of altruism needs to establish a clear link between the campaign's aims and objectives and the material interests of the individuals and groups that it hopes to mobilise. Although any political project will have an ethical dimension, maintaining people's long-term involvement requires more than merely moralistic exhortations to 'do the right thing'; it requires in addition the ability to clearly explain the web of connections between the movement's supporters and individuals and communities to whom they may feel only tenuously connected. An anti-racist group, for instance, can explain and expose the common class interests of white workers and their Bangladeshi neighbours and thus help to establish a firm basis for inter-racial solidarity. Such an approach not only helps to secure the commitment of members and campaigners, but it also implies an educational process that will help to equip them to act effectively and knowledgeably on their own initiative. This differs from the majority of charitable appeals, which may extol general humanitarian principles but without demanding more than a token gesture (generally financial) in return.

Sarah Moore, in her study of 'ribbon culture', describes how a lack of engagement is apparent in many 'awareness' campaigns. Most commonly associated with issues such as AIDs and breast cancer, the practice of wearing a coloured ribbon to publicise a particular problem has been investigated by Moore, who notes that ribbon-wearers generally have little knowledge of, or commitment to, the causes of which they claim to be 'aware'. She concludes instead, that apart from their fund-raising potential, the ribbons function as signifiers of the wearers' need to identity themselves as compassionate individuals and as branding devices for the charities involved. The ribbons cannot, therefore, be seen primarily as symbols of people's insight into specific issues.[30] The substitution of ritualistic displays of concern for informed involvement in social action is, as we have seen, one of the defining features of Bob Geldof's 'Aid' initiatives, and it clearly sets limits to the public's engagement in these campaigns. So although the desire to develop what Geldof terms a 'constituency of compassion' is certainly part of any large-scale movement to improve the lives of others, compassionate concern is not, in itself, sufficiently binding to hold together a movement of activists. Protest movements, furthermore, must look beyond their own ranks if they are to counter the influence of antagonistic groups and ideologies. They need to take into account the nature of the opposition – its strengths and weaknesses, its intentions, the social make-up of its adherents and the theoretical bases of its politics.

If activist-based movements are to remain relevant and effective, they must accommodate themselves to the shifting social terrain upon which they operate. This can be seen, to some degree, even in a largely top-down operation like Live 8, which was obliged to position itself as a directly political intervention in a struggle already shaped by several years of campaigning by NGOs, anti-capitalists, opponents of neo-liberal economic policies, and countless other forms of dissent, pressure and protest. Likewise, LMHR has had to take into account a number of significant social, political and cultural changes wrought since RAR ceased activity in 1981 and these have exerted a strong influence on the organisation's modes of operation. I have already touched on some of the technological and cultural shifts that have taken place in this period, but there have also been important developments in the nature of con-temporary racism and hence the tactics required to combat it. The most significant change in this respect is the central role now played by anti-Islamic sentiments in shaping perceptions of Muslim communities. To a large extent these notions are attributable to the impact of global instability and conflict on domestic politics. The 'war on terror' has been accompanied by a tendency to demonise Muslims, and this has been encouraged by Samuel Huntington's thesis that Islam and the 'west' are engaged in a 'clash of civilisations'.[31] The extent to which the spread of Islamophobia in Britain is due to the articulation at a local level of international power struggles, rather than racists' typical concern to defend 'their' community's perceived status, is debatable. It seems evident that the 'traditional' concerns of racism with skin colour and the allocation of scarce social resources, such as housing and jobs, are still relevant, although these can now sometimes be decked out in the more intellectually 'respectable' guise of a conflict between the west's secular values and the anti-Enlightenment theology of fundamentalist Islam. This interpretation of events has been echoed to some extent in official and media reactions to signs of increasing Muslim assertiveness. When Muslim (and, it should be noted, white) youth clashed with fascist groups and the police in northern English towns in 2001, the cause was often sought not in the levels of material deprivation experi-enced by all racial, ethnic and religious groups in the areas involved, but in Muslims' desire to segregate themselves in introverted and unas-similated communities, with little contact with the institutions and values of British society as a whole.[32] The validity of this analysis has been challenged, however, and, in a detailed report on the Bradford riots, Ludi Simpson, Professor of Population Research at the University of Manchester, argues that the composition of particular communities and the factors that cause them to change have little to do with the insularity of specific immigrant groups, and that social policy needs to be 'informed by a sociological and historical understanding of the class, housing, employment and educational dynamics of neighbourhood residential change.'[33]

The linkage between global concerns and domestic politics has been most clearly illustrated in the British government's commitment to waging full-scale war in Iraq and Afghanistan, whilst buttressing this on the home front through the adoption of an increasingly stringent 'national security' agenda. The terrorist attacks on the London transport system in July 2005 helped to crystallise a growing disquiet in government circles over Muslim extremism; this was voiced by leading Labour figures Jack Straw and David Blunkett, who publicised their unease regarding fanatical Muslim clerics and veil-wearing constituents.[34] More importantly, the international situation gave the New Labour government what one critic describes as 'a pretext for strengthening the internal power of the state itself'.[35]

In addition to an enhanced emphasis on the supposed cultural incompatibility between secular western values and Islam, concerns over immigration have been ratcheted up with respect to flows of refugees and asylum seekers from regions of instability and conflict, such as the Balkans and the Middle East,[36] and the growing numbers of migrants from newly acceded members of the European Union like the Czech Republic, Lithuania, Poland and Romania.[37]

As in the 1970s, a space on the far right of the political spectrum has been opened up through widespread disillusionment with Labour in office. The high hopes that greeted the election of the Blair administration in 1997 have given way to disappointment for many Labour supporters, as the government has enthusiastically embraced the socially divisive economic nostrums of neo-liberalism and became associated with a culture of 'spin' and dishonesty. Crucially, this culminated in Britain waging its ruinous war in Iraq on the back of doctored evidence.[38] Disenchantment with New Labour is, however, only one aspect of a more far-reaching sense of disaffection with orthodox politics as a whole. Historically low turnouts at general elections, especially among young and working-class voters, are a revealing symptom of this mood,[39] and it is a development which suggests that large numbers of people are finding it difficult to legitimise through the ballot box a political establishment that seems indifferent towards the aspirations and concerns of ordinary people. The BNP has been able to capitalise on this mood, and just as Labour's rightward drift on immigration during the 1960s and 1970s played into the hands of the far-right, so New Labour's tough rhetoric on asylum seekers and its attempts to present itself as the saviour of 'British values' have conceded a great deal to those who would like to push such ideas and policies to extreme conclusions.[40] Meanwhile, even erstwhile defenders of multiculturalism – such as the Chair of the Commission for Racial Equality, Sir Trevor Phillips – have evoked fears of segregation and the creation of US-style ghettos, and these arguments have been picked up throughout the media. One columnist writing in the *Independent* went so far as to declare that multiculturalism is 'an excuse for tokenism, laziness, patronisation, ghettoisation, simmering resentment, poverty, alienation, fundamentalism and terrorism'.[41]

Like New Labour, the BNP has undergone a face-lift. The party's retreat from the nakedly fascistic tactics and pronouncements of the NF, and its cultivation of a respectable public persona marks a shift towards a more 'constitutional' approach to politics. The BNP's adoption of a strategy that focuses on elections, rather than militant confrontation with its opponents, protects the party from exposure to the kinds of unevenly balanced conflicts with anti-racists that put paid to the National Front. The decision to pursue an electoralist line has seen dozens of BNP councillors elected, mainly in the north and midlands, but also a significant number in the party's strongholds in east London and Essex.[42] In achieving these gains, the BNP has undoubtedly benefited from the tendency throughout the political establishment to drag political debate rightwards, especially on issues such as immigration and national security.

The situation in the first decade of the twenty-first century, then, bears a resemblance to that in the 1970s, but it is also marked by substantial differences. It is against this background that we need to consider LMHR's chief aims and objectives, which have been described as follows: 'To create a national movement against racism and fascism, via the music scene, involving music fans and musicians. To be the cultural wing of the anti-fascist movement, to help undermine the BNP. To take up wider questions of racism in society, particularly those relating to music and culture.'[43] It is to LMHR's version of cultural politics that we will now turn.

RAR's main musical props were, as we have seen, punk rock and reggae. In this relationship punk supplied not simply a soundtrack, but also a widely diffused set of attitudes and informal structures through which RAR could disseminate its message. RAR didn't simply latch onto a ready-made subcultural milieu, however, but also contributed to its development through staging and promoting concerts, allowing bands opportunities to perform, establishing a strong relationship with the music press and so on. The absence of a subcultural equivalent to punk rock is one of the most obvious factors distinguishing LMHR from RAR, and it raises the question of how far the latter organisation can lay claim to its predecessor's mantle. Dave Renton addresses this point in his history of the ANL, where he cautions us against fetishising particular musical forms as innately radical. Although he maintains that '[t]here was an intimate relationship between the music of Rock Against Racism and the politics of the Anti-Nazi League', Renton also declares: 'The meaning of any musical style is set in dialogue with its audience; it is contextual and changes over time.' And he illustrates his argument with a direct reference to punk: 'The "anarchism" of the Sex Pistols meant something more in 1977 than it did in 1981 – after Malcolm McLaren and the militant cynicism of *The Great Rock and Roll Swindle*.'[44] Following Renton, then, it would be unrealistic to expect a modern-day RAR to replicate the same musical coalition that characterised its first incarnation.[45]

So, although LMHR concerts do not benefit from the raw energy and radical charge of the punk/reggae axis, they offer a platform for a range of musical forms that reflect more accurately the immense changes that have overtaken popular music since the 1970s. This cultural mix is suggested in LMHR's adaptation of the RAR slogan from which it derived its name. Thus, 'Reggae, Soul, Rock 'n' Roll, Jazz, Funk and Punk' has been replaced by 'Rock – Hip-hop – Bhangra – Drum n Bass – Indie – Reggae – R&B – Punk – Grime – Jazz ... our music', a litany that is suggestive of major changes in the nature of popular music since RAR's heyday.[46] The inclusion of bhangra confirms the importance of south-Asian influences on modern music, but as we noted above, this represents only one part of a wider process of ethnic diversification within the music scene that has blurred the distinctions between 'black' and 'white'.

The relatively sharp ethnic and racial distinctions that could still be discerned in popular music in the 1970s are arguably less clear now, but this does not mean that colour bias has been eliminated. In a *Guardian* interview in March 2008, for instance, black British singer Estelle Swaray criticised the music industry's tendency to promote white singers such as Duffy and Adele at the expense of black performers. Her frustration at being side-lined in favour of practitioners of 'blue-eyed soul' prompted Estelle's move to New York, where she received a more positive reception.[47] But besides the continuing problem of racial prejudice within the music scene, centrifugal processes also operate via the technologies and media through which modern popular culture is generated.

Ausaf Abbas has commented on the extent to which means of communication such as multi-channel TV, internet blogs, and social networking and file-sharing sites provide opportunities for even the most marginal social groups to consolidate themselves around particular 'identities' and interests. According to Abbas, this proliferation of 'special interest' niches and enclaves has accentuated tendencies towards social atomisation.[48] So if modern technologies have provided means through which cultural hybridity can be advanced, they can also encourage the kind of fragmentation against which united front campaigns can act as a unifying influence.

To a greater extent than RAR – whose cultural boundaries were relatively restricted, and which was active in an environment in which many fewer 'subaltern' voices had filtered through into the public sphere – LMHR has had to negotiate the contradictions of multiculturalism. Although the campaign still appeals to ideals of inter-racial fraternity on the basis of a shared participation in a multicultural music scene, the concept of 'difference' now enjoys a wider currency than in the 1970s. Whilst LMHR still celebrates ethnic and racial diversity in opposition to the idea that 'British culture' is solely a product of the country's allegedly 'indigenous' population (and a heavily mythologised, ahistorical and de-classed version of this population at that),[49] multiculturalism has acquired connotations beyond these racialised categories. As Tariq Modood argues *vis-à-vis* the Muslim experience:

> Indeed, it is best to see the development of racial explicitness and Muslim assertiveness as part of a wider socio-political climate which is not confined to race and culture or non-white minorities. Feminism, gay pride, Quebecois nationalism and the revival of Scottishness are some prominent examples of these new identity movements which have come to be an important feature in many countries, especially those in which class politics has declined. This means that our basic concept of civil rights or civic equality has been supplemented by the concept of equality as 'difference', by the right to have one's 'difference' recognized and supported in the public sphere.[50]

But when disarticulated from the concept of power, this vision of 'equality through diversity' can be readily assimilated by racists and other authoritarians, who may demand segregated spaces within which to 'celebrate' their 'own' heritage.[51] Embedding multiculturalism within an active anti-hegemonic critique affords a way out of this impasse. A united front demands the search for commonalities rather than the endless pursuit of new forms of differentiation and it obliges its members to comprehend and confront those forces against which they are jointly opposed. It is this rejection of abstract theorising in favour of Marx's 'practical-critical activity' that shaped RAR's approach to multiculturalism, and it is a sufficiently adaptable principle to provide guidance through the contemporary thickets of identity politics.

RAR's mission, it is clear, has altered through its translation into a twenty-first-century setting. One such change can be found in the reduced emphasis, in LMHR, of RAR's deeply embedded commitment to a radical visual culture. RAR drew direct inspiration from the aesthetics of early twentieth-century modernism, 1960s pop art and the often Dadaesque cut and paste techniques of punk rock, and its design team were concerned with exploring the boundaries of their craft, but LMHR's style is less experimental. Although certain components of RAR and ANL iconography have been appropriated by the newer campaign, they act as branding devices, rather than as elements within a deliberately challenging graphic identity. The relatively understated quality of LMHR's imagery can be attributed in large part to the organisation's status as a carefully calculated intervention on the part of the ANL (and later Unite Against Fascism),[52] as opposed to a largely spontaneous act of guerrilla activism by culturally savvy left-wingers. LMHR was founded by anti-racist activists with a desire to see popular music re-enlisted in the fight against fascism, but without the personal commitment to their own role as cultural producers that characterised the likes of Red Saunders, Roger Huddle, Syd Shelton, Ruth Gregory and David Widgery. For both LMHR and RAR popular music has been fundamental to their existence, but RAR's mission was always defined more broadly; not simply as an anti-racist initiative that used rock music as a vehicle to carry a political message, but as a contribution to radical culture in its own right. As David Widgery explained in *Beating Time*:

> It took to the end of 1976 for the little RAR group to hammer out its ideas and consolidate a core of visual artists, musicians and writers who could drive the project ahead. But for that group the feeling of fear and passivity against the Front's advance was over, at least in our heads; we were going to strike back kung-fu, rub-a-dub, surrealist style. RAR's resources were small and we still participated in our other personas as committed lefties in the direct confrontations with the National Front. It was a piece of double-time, with the musical and the political confrontations on simultaneous but separate tracks and difficult to mix.[53]

One manifestation of this distinction between RAR and LMHR, is that Love Music Hate Racism does not have an equivalent to *Temporary*

Hoarding. More than a 'house magazine', the journal provided a medium through which RAR's writers, designers and assorted propagandists and enthusiasts could argue their politics and engage in debate with the wider movement. *Temporary Hoarding*'s success lay not simply in its role as a means of communication and organisation, but as a channel through which racism in Britain could be contextualised, debated and theorised. LMHR defines its remit more narrowly than RAR. According to a leading LMHR figure: 'Perhaps because of the times it grew up in, RAR sometimes took up issues beyond racism and fascism, e.g. sexism, Northern Ireland, etc, which we don't.'[54] Such a statement might seem to imply a less rigorous exploration of the social background to contemporary racism and fascism than RAR achieved, but against this we need to reiterate certain points: first is the necessarily restricted scope of any united front, which is deliberately formulated to secure the widest possible level of support; but beyond this lies the network of political, social and cultural bodies associated with the alliance, which together will have much more expansive aims. The crux of the matter is that a united front does not have to do *everything*. As with RAR, attendance at LMHR events allows participants to explore their views on race and culture both directly and indirectly, and it provides a point of contact with a range of organisations and campaigns that are involved in multiple forms of political and agitational activity extending beyond anti-racism and anti-fascism; a situation which echoes the mass anti-fascist mobilisations of the 1970s.[55]

We should beware of letting our recognition of the differences between RAR and later anti-racist movements descend into a nostalgic yearning for a more radical past, as if RAR provides a kind of 'gold standard' against which other movements need to valorise themselves. As I suggested at the start of this section, different contexts demand different responses. Having once discovered the potency of the union between anti-racist politics and popular music it would seem perverse not to exploit this once again in the face of a racist revival. To delay acting in the hope that a purely spontaneous movement will arise would seem not merely misguided, but even irresponsible. One of the advantages of hindsight is that it allows activists to apply to current conditions principles that have been tested in the past, and they can, to some extent, skip developmental stages that were previously unavoidable. LMHR is, after all, working in an environment shaped by RAR and it is able to appeal to people on the basis of their previous experience of music and politics. In this sense, then, LMHR is in a more advantageous position than RAR, because it can recall the example of the 1970s and draw on the memories and life histories of individuals who were involved in anti-racist politics at the time. Thus the speakers at UAF events include people like Peter Hain, Jerry Dammers, Ken Livingstone and Gurinder Chadha, while LMHR gigs frequently feature ex-RAR supporters such as the Buzzcocks, Mick Jones (Clash bass guitarist), the Beat and Neville Staple (of the Specials). The way in which LMHR has been able to capitalise on RAR's heritage is suggested in a *Guardian* article from March 2008, which reports LMHR's participation in a programme to distribute musical instruments to prisoners. The governor of Brixton Prison, Paul McDowell, explains his enthusiasm for the Jail Guitar Doors project in terms of his youthful involvement in antiracist politics: 'The roots of this go back all the way to my involvement as a teenager in the Anti-Nazi League and on the periphery of RAR.' Jail Guitar Doors also has a link to the RAR experience through the late Joe Strummer, a carnival stalwart in whose memory the initiative has been established.[56]

One of the most spectacular features of anti-racist agitation in the 1970s, but which is largely absent today, was large-scale physical confrontation between racists and their organised political opponents. The great mass demonstrations such as occurred at Southall and Lewisham, and the countless skirmishes elsewhere across the country, were a direct response to the NF's politics of aggression and their determination to intimidate immigrant communities by staging marches and meetings in areas with large black and Asian populations. As we have seen, RAR, in association with the ANL, was part of an anti-fascist front that aimed to physically prevent the far-right from mobilising in public spaces. In this atmosphere RAR gigs became frequent targets of fascist hooligans, and physical security was consequently a vital consideration.[57] Although racially motivated attacks are unfortunately still common, and high levels of racist violence are linked with the activities of the BNP and other racist groups in particular areas,[58] the BNP's emphasis on elections has shifted the focus away from physical force. Inevitably, LMHR has shadowed this change in strategy and although – along with its allies – it still aims to restrict fascism's freedom to flourish, this does not primarily entail confronting fascists in spatially bounded areas such as public squares and shopping precincts, but rather establishing a counterpresence in institutionally and culturally defined arenas like the education system and the mass media. Racist discourse is now so heavily freighted with assumptions and arguments to do with culture that antiracist politics must address these issues as a matter of urgency. This does not mean that the threat of physical violence is now absent from the calculations of fascist groups – as assaults and campaigns of harassment against anti-fascists illustrate[59] – but it does confront organisations like UAF and LMHR with the necessity of developing counter-cultural strategies that go beyond the field of popular music.

Both Live 8 and Love Music Hate Racism represent contemporary iterations of past campaigns, and both have attempted to articulate the original ideas of their precursors, but modified to suit new conditions. Unlike in 1984–85, when Band Aid and Live Aid led the way in mobilising popular sentiment in support of starving Africans, Live 8 in 2005 piggy-backed an existing movement. Although Geldof's later intervention was explicitly political rather than simply humanitarian, Live 8 reproduced a number of the earlier campaign's features. Notably, concert audiences were still posited as passive consumers of politically inspired entertainment, while the serious business of engaging in direct action was restricted to prominent figureheads such as Geldof and Bono. In both 1985 and 2005, popular music was used to engage a mass audience and to dramatise and celebrate their shared hopes and concerns. In both cases, however, black artists were consciously marginalised by Geldof, whose expansive vision of building a 'constituency of compassion' lacked any means to articulate the links between localised struggles and global issues concerning the unequal distribution of both wealth and – crucially – social power.

Love Music Hate Racism has tried to revive RAR's *modus operandi* of building a mass anti-racist movement based on popular music. Lacking the wide-ranging subcultural networks generated by punk rock, LMHR has, from the start, had to mobilise through different channels. In some respects LMHR is more advantageously situated than RAR, having been able to draw on the older movement's experience as well as support from a more cosmopolitan music scene than RAR was dealing with. To this extent LMHR's appeal is potentially wider than RAR's. The BNP's cultivation of a less extremist image and its move towards 'constitutional' politics has necessitated a corresponding shift on the part of the anti-racist movement. One by-product of this change in tactics is that the large-scale physical confrontations that were a strong feature of anti-fascist activity in the 1970s are largely absent now. If LMHR has benefited from some of the developments in popular music since the 1970s, it has arguably lacked the cultural assertiveness and inventiveness of RAR, even though culture-bound notions of civilisational conflict and 'equality as difference' have become increasingly common in the public domain.

Notes

1 Good places to look for this kind of overview are: Denselow, *When the Music's Over* and Garofalo, *Rockin' the Boat*.

2 Widgery, *Beating Time*, p. 116.

3 Nicky Tesco, interview (5 December 2000).

4 Nicky Tesco, interview (5 December 2000); and Geoff Hare, 'Popular music on French radio and television', in Steve Cannon and Hugh Dauncy (eds), *Popular Music in France from Chanson to Techno* (Ashgate, Aldershot, 2003).

5 See, for instance, the collection of essays in: Ellen Koskoff (ed.), *Music Cultures in the United States: An introduction* (Routledge, London, 2005).

6 Mike Davis, *City of Quartz: Excavating the future in Los Angeles* (Vintage, London, 1992), pp. 87–88.

7 One of the most controversial, but also influential, contributions to this process was Paul Simon's *Graceland* album, which mixed South African musical styles with 'American' genres such as bluegrass and zydeco. Simon's decision to break the UN's cultural boycott of South Africa in order to collaborate with South African musicians in preparing this record provoked a mixed reaction. Some critics accused him of simply appropriating African music for his own commercial gain, while others noted that the boycott didn't distinguish between the apartheid state and black musicians who were being denied access to a global audience. For a balanced discussion see: Louise Meintjes, 'Paul Simon's Graceland, South Africa and the mediation of musical meaning', in Simon Frith (ed.), *Popular Music: Critical concepts in media and cultural studies*, Volume IV, Music and Identity (Routledge, London, 2004).

8 Denis-Constant Martin, 'Music beyond apartheid?', in Garofalo, *Rockin' the Boat*.

9 Cited in Hutnyk, *Critique of Exotica*, p. 27.

10 Rehan Hyder, *Brimful of Asia: Negotiating ethnicity on the UK music scene* (Ashgate, Aldershot, 2004), p. 51.

11 Naomi Klein, *No Logo* (Flamingo, London, 2000), ch 3.

12 Hutnyk, *Critique of Exotica*, pp. 27–28.

13 For a discussion of these issues see: Roy Shuker, *Understanding Popular Music* (Routledge, London, 2001), ch 4; and David Murphy, 'Where does world music come from? Globalization Afropop and the question of cultural identity', in Ian Biddle and Vanessa Knights (eds), *Music, National Identity and the Politics of Location: Between the global and the local* (Ashgate, Aldershot, 2007).

14 Esther Leslie, *Walter Benjamin's Arcades Project*, www.militantesthetix. co.uk/waltbenj/yarcades.html, downloaded 27 June 2007.

15 Rupa Huq, *Beyond Subculture: Pop, youth and identity in a postcolonial world* (Routledge, London, 2006), ch 4.

16 Widgery, *Beating Time*, p. 114.

17 These figures are cited on Bob Geldof's official website: www.bobgeldof. info/Charity/liveaid.html, downloaded 29 December 2007.

18 John Street, Seth Hague and Heather Savigny, 'The voice of the people? Musicians as political actors', *Cultural Politics*, 4:1 (March 2008), p. 11.

19 Widgery, *Beating Time*, p. 114.

20 Ibid.

21 George Monbiot, 'Bards of the powerful', http://arts.guardian.co.uk/live8/ story/0,,1510824,00.html, downloaded 22 October 2007.

22 Bob Geldof, 'Geldof's year', http://arts.guardian.co.uk/live8/story/0,,1674 290,00.html, downloaded 22 October 2007.

23 Street, Hague and Savigny, 'Playing to the crowd'.

24 'Taking on the multinationals in Bolivia', *International Socialism Journal*, 2:111 (Summer 2006).

25 Street, Hague and Savigny, 'The voice of the people?', p. 19.

26 Geldof, *Is That It?*, p. 365.

27 Geldof, 'Geldof's year'.

28 Street, Hague and Savigny, 'Playing to the crowd', p. 283.

29 Street, Hague and Savigny, 'The voice of the people?', p. 19.

30 Sarah E.H. Moore, *Ribbon Culture: Charity, compassion and public awareness* (Palgrave Macmillan, Basingstoke, 2008).

31 Samuel P. Huntington, *The Clash of Civilizations and the Remaking of World Order* (The Free Press, London, 2002).

32 Tariq Modood, 'British Muslims and the politics of multiculturalism', in Tariq Modood, Anna Triandafyllidou and Richard Zapata-Barrero (eds), *Multiculturalism, Muslims and Citizenship: A European approach* (Routledge, London, 2006).

33 Ludi Simpson, 'Statistics of racial segregation: measures, evidence and policy', *Urban Studies*, 41:3 (March 2004), pp. 661–681.

34 Chris Gray, 'Blunkett changes entry rules for Muslim clerics', www. independent.co.uk/news/uk/politics/blunkett-changes-entry-rules-for-muslim-clerics-621336.html, downloaded 1 April 2008. 'Straw's veil comments spark anger', http://news.bbc.co.uk/1/hi/uk_politics/5410472.stm, downloaded 1 April 2008.

35 Steven Kettell, *Dirty Politics? New Labour, British democracy and the invasion of Iraq* (Zed Books, London, 2006), p. 55.

36 Mark Cutts et al, *The State of the World's Refugees 2000: Fifty years of humanitarian action* (Oxford University Press, Oxford, 2000). Nara Merheb et al, *The State of the World's Refugees 2006: Human displacement in the new millennium* (Oxford University Press, Oxford, 2006).

37 Immigration statistics for the period 1991–2006 are available as: *First_ Release_Tables_91–06.xls*, available at www.statistics.gov.uk/statbase/ Product.asp?vlnk=15053, downloaded 25 March 2008.

38 Kettell, *Dirty Politics?*.

39 Voter turnout in general elections, already low at 71.4 per cent when New Labour took office in 1997, nose-dived to 59.4 per cent in 2001 and

recovered only slightly to stand at 61.4 per cent in 2005. These latter two results constitute two out of the three lowest turnouts since 1918 (when many troops were still abroad and hence unable to participate). Disaffection is most evident amongst young people between the ages of 18 and 24, of whom only 37 per cent voted in 2005. See: *Election 2005: turnout. How many, who and why?* (The Electoral Commission, London, 2005).

40 For a discussion of the Labour Party's stance on immigration see: Don Flynn, 'Immigration controls and citizenship in the political rhetoric of New Labour', in Elia Zureik and Mark B. Salter (eds), *Global Surveillance and Policing: Borders, security, identity* (Willan Publishing, Uffcolme, 2005).

41 Deborah Orr, 'Why we should ditch black history month', *Independent* (5 October 2005).

42 See the table at: www.uaf.org.uk/news.asp?choice=70503.

43 Lee Billingham, personal communication (27 February 2008).

44 Renton, *When We Touched the Sky*, pp. 181–182.

45 In a similar vein to Nicky Tesco, cited earlier in this chapter, Red Saunders and Roger Huddle argued in 2000 that changes in the nature of popular music would influence any attempt to revive the RAR formula: Red Saunders and Roger Huddle, interview (4 June 2000).

46 One thing that has been lost in translation is the metre of the original slogan, which could be rhythmically chanted.

47 Esther Addley and Alex Macpherson, 'Estelle attacks "blindness to black talent"', *Guardian* (28 March 2008). See also: Rupa Huq, 'Soul with blue eyes', *Guardian* (29 March 2008).

48 Ausaf Abbas, interview (23 March 2008).

49 The BNP's version of this myth is promulgated through their website. The party's Mission Statement, which contains a section on culture, is available at: www.bnp.org.uk/2008/02/28/mission-statement-2/, downloaded 30 March 2008.

50 Tariq Modood, 'British Muslims and the politics of multiculturalism', in Modood, Triandafyllidou and Zapata-Barrero, *Multiculturalism, Muslims and Citizenship*.

51 Hassan Mahamdallie, 'Racism: myths and realities', *International Socialism Journal*, 2:95 (Summer 2002). The BNP's willingness to exploit the idea that it simply represents another downtrodden ethnic community has found expression through its 'Ethnic Liaison Committee', which seeks to cultivate contacts with other (carefully chosen and vetted) racial and ethnic groups. See this article from the *Searchlight* website: Nick Lowles, 'Sleeping with the enemy: Griffin ponders black membership', www.searchlightmagazine. com/index.php?link=template&story=61, downloaded 30 March 2008.

52 Unite Against Fascism was set up during 2003–04, as an attempt to broaden the basis of anti-BNP activity. It has gained the support of a wide range of trade unions, political organisations and campaigns. Both LMHR and the ANL quickly affiliated to the campaign.

53 Widgery, *Beating Time*, p. 43.

54 Lee Billingham, personal communication (27 February 2008).

55 One of the venues for this interaction, unavailable to RAR at the time, is the Left Field at the annual Glastonbury Festival. This trade union sponsored portion of the main festival site has been a regular feature since 2003 and has regularly hosted Love Music Hate Racism events.

56 Duncan Campbell, 'After Presley and Cash, Alabama 3 get prison blues', *Guardian* (22 March 2008).

57 Ausaf Abbas recalls a gig in Clapham, south London, where the venue was smashed up by NF-supporting skinheads, who also attacked audience members: Ausaf Abbas, interview (23 March 2008). See also David Widgery's description of the close-quarters encounters between RAR and the far-right: Widgery, *Beating Time*, pp. 79–81.

58 Paul Harris, 'Far right plot to provoke race riots', *Observer* (3 June 2001); Paul Stokes, 'White extremists blamed for race riots', www.telegraph.co.uk/news/main.jhtml?xml=/news/2001/05/29/nriot29.xml, downloaded 2 April 2008.

59 Anti-fascist magazine *Searchlight* has reported on the pro-Nazi 'Redwatch' website, which carries personal details of activists opposed to racism. See: Nick Lowles, 'It's time to get Watty! – British nazi admits to running Redwatch', www.searchlightmagazine.com/index.php?link=template&story=173, downloaded 2 April 2008.

7

Conclusions

My decision to discuss the cultural politics of RAR has been motivated by a conviction that the movement's aesthetic and political dimensions were enmeshed in ways that few commentators have allowed for. All too often, RAR's politics and its relationships with the SWP and other organisations and individuals have been interpreted via crude assumptions regarding the left and movements of popular protest. Insufficient attention has been paid to the specific historical context in which RAR operated and the political and cultural traditions that informed its activities. I have tried to address these issues in my study and I would propose a number of conclusions on this basis.

Fundamentally, RAR was a creative response to the profound social and political crisis that gripped Britain in the 1970s and which disoriented much of the left. One consequence of this situation – the 'shift in emphasis' in the SWP, from industrial to political struggles – opened up a space within which socialists could build an anti-racist movement rooted in popular culture. The SWP's ability to promote this development was helped by its emphasis on the importance of rank and file organisation and its rejection of the pro-Soviet perspectives of much of the left. A generation of militants in and around the SWP, who combined revolutionary politics with a genuine love for popular music, provided many of RAR's leading cadres. Meanwhile, the upsurge in radical trends in youth cultures such as punk and reggae, supplied a channel through which this small number of activists could communicate with much larger numbers of campaigners and sympathisers. But RAR was more than an ideological and organisational force; it engaged in cultural practices, such as the production of innovative visual propaganda, which were representative of the politico-cultural ideals of the movement's founders.

Although the SWP provided vital ideological and logistical support for RAR, it was not the sole source of RAR's finance, politics or personnel. For good practical and political reasons the SWP neither wanted direct operational control of RAR nor could exercise it. Despite the assertions of some critics, the aims and objectives of the left cannot be reduced to schemes for bureaucratic dominance over competing political tendencies.[1] Apart from being self-defeating – for an over-emphasis on bureaucratic procedures tends to isolate the left from those over whom it would like to exert real influence – such a strategy may bring with it organisational burdens that can swamp the resources of a small group.[2] It seems clear that RAR, insofar as it stimulated the self-activity of broad layers of activists that lay beyond the confines of the established left, was motivated by the spirit, if not the letter, of the 'united front method'. Recent research, particularly that conducted at the UEA, has helped to re-establish the importance of pre-existing cultural and political networks in providing much of RAR's organisational scaffolding, as well as access to broad swathes of individuals and organisations that were willing to sign up to the campaign's ideals. The relative weakness of revolutionary socialism in the mid- to late 1970s set limits to the tasks that could be undertaken by handful of dedicated activists, and it certainly ruled out the kind of direct challenge to the reformist leadership of the working class envisaged by Trotsky in his writings on Germany. Nevertheless, RAR's principled pragmatism answered the needs of a modestly sized campaigning body, which lacked the administrative clout of larger organisations such as the Communist Party or the Labour Party.

It can be argued that a number of SWP members, including some of its leadership, were unsympathetic towards the cultural milieu in which RAR was active. Syd Shelton and Ruth Gregory certainly feel that the relationship between the two organisations could be tense, but that the SWP was in no position to simply assimilate a movement with RAR's social and ideological complexion. However, if some party members were unsure of RAR, many also devoted considerable time and energy to building the movement and RAR benefited enormously from the party's support. But of course RAR was not the only anti-racist campaign active during the 1970s; it worked closely alongside the ANL, particularly in organising the massive carnivals that helped to build a mood of defiance against resurgent fascism. Although both the ANL and RAR were partners in the struggle, they embodied different approaches to building an anti-racist and anti-fascist current in British political and social life. As we have seen, the ANL provided a more realistic means than RAR for the SWP to re-engage with the labour movement following a period of retreat and realignment on the left. This judgement does not flow from any lack of appreciation of the value of RAR in the anti-racist struggle, but rather from a realistic assessment of the different roles played by RAR and the ANL. RAR was necessarily a relatively narrow campaign, which had only a tangential connection with the institutions of organised labour; the ANL on the other hand was not limited by a particular set of cultural enthusiasms and it appealed directly to a broad range of social and political interests, including trade unions and important community groups. It is largely for this reason that the ANL was more prominent than RAR in the political calculations of the SWP.

Just as racism within the music industry inspired the creation of RAR, it also helped to define the cultural content of the new movement, and this, rather than inherent anti-Asian sentiment on the left, helped to determine the limited scope of RAR's musical repertoire. After all, the central irony behind Eric Clapton's racist outburst in 1976 was that he had built a successful career through performing music informed, in one way or another, by the life experiences of people of African descent. But if Clapton's onstage histrionics helped RAR to refine their cultural act, there were other, more sinister influences pushing RAR towards punk and reggae.

The racist right had long struggled to define its own cultural identity, but in the mid-1970s some fascists were staking a claim to popular music: they not only attempted to brand punk rock as a new Aryan folk music, but also – in an apparently perverse act of appropriation – they gravitated towards reggae music. But maybe this was not so odd after all. What many alienated and desperate white youth will have related to were certain of reggae's commanding narratives: of struggle and ultimate redemption; of the fighting spirit of an embattled people, striving to carve out an area of beauty and pleasure in the midst of exile and rejection. Such themes must have appealed to young white people who felt let down by the institutions of their 'own' society; but how humiliating it must also have been for this racist fringe to realise that their self-image was composed in part from cultural achievements stolen from black Caribbean youth. Those among the NF's leadership who at least tolerated such cultural miscegenation may have reached the conclusion that the aesthetic landscape of young white people was shaped by cosmopolitan forces over which they had no control, and that they were better off tolerating this than trying to inspire reluctant white youngsters with their own insipid tastes in 'indigenous' music. This attitude of half-hearted toleration, combined with ignorant bigotry, informs Martin Webster's remarks in 1978: 'There again, it depends whether you're prepared to absorb their kind of music. I enjoy *some*, not all black music. But I could live without it . . . No, I'm not interested in destroying rock 'n' roll . . . I just don't want MY British people to end up committing biological suicide – genocide.'[3]

If black culture was too deeply embedded in the lives of white youth for the likes of John Tyndall and Martin Webster to excise, it was part of RAR's intent to deny this cultural territory to the enemy. At the very least, RAR could confront white music fans with the implicit logic of their musical preferences and ask them if it was not more truly joyful and radical to embrace the multicultural reality of modern Britain, than to stay locked into the dour and regressive fantasies of white supremacy.

But the ironic homage paid to black culture by some racists offered no protection against the intimidation being routinely visited upon immigrant communities by the far-right. Much less did it impede the apparent onslaught against black culture being carried out by sections of the British state. As we have seen, negative attitudes among the police towards black Caribbean communities and the enforcement of a tough 'law and order' agenda – directed in part against cultural events like the Notting Hill Carnival – helped to confirm Jamaican music as a key locus for anti-racist agitation and propaganda. RAR felt duty-bound to demonstrate its practical and cultural solidarity with the black victims of such state-sponsored oppression.

A further constraint on RAR's cultural and ethnic appeal arose from its status as a focused anti-racist campaign rather than a political party fighting on many fronts. Paul Gilroy has noted that anti-racism is a largely white preoccupation[4] and RAR's emphasis on addressing itself mainly to white youth reflects this reality. In communicating with its audience RAR needed to develop a cultural identity with which significant numbers of young whites could empathise, and here again the movement's founders were confronted with the reality that in Britain, in 1976, this meant leaning heavily on forms of popular music that could trace their heritage back to African sources.

But having argued the case for the choices RAR made in terms of its cultural 'offer', we should not overstate the narrowness of the campaign's ethnic appeal, particularly with regard to young Asians, a number of whom *were* active in RAR. The organisation made efforts to build links with the Asian community through means other than popular culture, but, given the circumstances of the time, pop music could not provide a major point of contact between the British left and Asian people. It is apparent, however, that the atmosphere of inclusion and resistance that RAR and other anti-racist and anti-fascist struggles engendered could boost the morale of Asian communities and encourage them to assert their own interests.

It has been argued that RAR blunted the radicalism of punk rock, but the dispute over some punks' use of Nazi symbolism exposed a conflict between a largely 'aestheticised' approach to the issue and one that was informed by a combination of cultural activism and 'hard politics'. The former relied upon the shock effect of punk's profanity in jolting people into an awareness of the dangerous snares that 'common sense' had laid for them. It was a blow against complacency, but one struck from outside, by an enlightened elite. The latter position was more pragmatic. It counselled against the danger of legitimising the symbols of fascism, since this provided a cover for race hatred. Rather than shocking people into an awareness of the 'spectacular' nature of late capitalism, RAR invited them to participate in activities that questioned, and hopefully undermined, some of its ideological assumptions. The former approach was largely about delivering semiological bombshells and it could be pursued with little regard for the practicalities of building and maintaining a stable anti-racist coalition. It thus assumed the existence of a critical gap between a radical intelligentsia and the benumbed masses. The latter approach was less histrionic, but it meant challenging bourgeois ideology at the point at which it was generated and maintained – in the everyday lives of ordinary people. As such, it assumed that the power to loosen the grip of racist ideas lay in the hands of these selfsame people and that what was required was leadership rather than ultimatums.

Contrary to certain interpretations, RAR cannot be understood as a product of a single, authoritative version of Marxist aesthetic theory applied to the realm of popular culture. The contrasts between RAR and the folk revival are suggestive of clear ideological divisions within Marxism, and they confirm that the ways in which Marxists have enacted their ideas have been shaped by events in the world at large. Thus, we cannot grasp the significance of the post-war folk revival without also considering the influence of the Cold War, and we cannot separate RAR from the state of British capitalism in the 1970s and the collapse of consensus politics. It is also the case that RAR was informed by the flowering of 'humanist Marxism' promoted by the rise of the New Left in the 1950s and 1960s, and that the emphasis that theorists such as Raymond Williams and E.P. Thompson placed on culture paved the way for later experiments in politically engaged cultural activism. The New Left's concern to rescue the lives of the 'common people' from the 'enormous condescension of posterity' proved inspiring to a younger generation of socialists dedicated to intervening in struggles at the grassroots of society, and to utilising the tools provided by popular culture (however debased by commerce) in their fight.

Many (but by no means all) of RAR's leading activists may have been Marxists, but those who were in the SWP represented not only a

Trotskyist perspective, but a dissident, state capitalist, variant at that. Far from expressing a monolithic Marxist approach to culture, RAR broke ranks with most of the left by choosing to orient itself on the products of the capitalist music industry – the phrase 'popular culture' in this context pertaining to patterns of consumption rather than conditions of production. Some RAR activists, like David Widgery, could sometimes exaggerate the revolutionary potential of popular music and of the subcultures that coalesced around it, but nevertheless RAR successfully negotiated the difficult terrain between the worlds of musical appreciation and political commitment. In doing so the organisation distinguished itself from other groups and individuals on the left – such as the Communist Party or Music for Socialism – that tended to promote overly elitist interpretations of Marxist cultural theory. Roger Huddle attests that the traditions with which RAR identified were at their most potent when associated with social struggles. Thus, the antidote to political passivity, or merely aestheticised posturing, lay not simply in regurgitating the forms of early twentieth-century modernism, but in attempting to reproduce something of its character, by harnessing popular culture to a movement of popular protest.

The continuity between art and politics postulated by Huddle and others helps us to distinguish between RAR and other causes that have enlisted popular music in pursuance of their aims. This certainly sets RAR apart from Bob Geldof's 'Aid' projects, which shared a number of cultural assumptions with the older campaign, although not its orientation on the self-activity of its supporters. In a sense, then, RAR stood between the attitude of the folk revival – which decried any accommodation with commercial pop music – and the various 'Aid' initiatives – which saw commercial success as the main determinant of an artist's worth to the cause. Viewed from this angle, Love Music Hate Racism therefore seems close to the spirit of its predecessor, although this is an imperfect match and a number of factors militate against any attempt to simply replicate the RAR model. Apart from the impossibility of mimicking the precise blend of social, economic and political conditions that gave rise to RAR, we also need to appreciate the fortunate coincidence between its organisers' ambition to build a 'rank and file movement against the racist poison in rock music' and the arrival on the scene of a subculture – punk rock – that embodied the kind of 'do-it-yourself' attitude that could articulate this ambition on a large scale. This is not to say that grassroots cultural activism is no longer possible, but rather that the means through which it operates and the technological, political and cultural resources at the disposal of activists in the early twenty-first century are radically different from those available over 30 years ago. Among the most vital of RAR's human resources, it must be noted, was the generation of cultural activists, such as Red Saunders, Roger Huddle and David Widgery, that helped to give the movement its unique identity and political character.

It is at least arguable that the racially and ethnically diverse character of so much modern pop music owes something to the pioneering work carried out by RAR. It is anachronistic, however, to project into the past developments that have occurred since 1981, and to take RAR to task for not predicting or encouraging them; this is particularly true of the increasingly visible and audible Asian presence within the popular-cultural sphere, including dance music and film.[5] RAR was in no position to anticipate cultural trends that have taken over 20 years to assume their present shape.

We must recall that RAR fought as part of an alliance, which brought together vast numbers of people, whether as members and supporters of organised campaigns, or as committed and concerned individuals. The extent and depth of this movement's victory over British Nazism was admitted by Martin Webster, who acknowledged that the NF was prevented from marching, recruiting, or effectively campaigning due to the relentless opposition it faced from anti-fascists.[6] However troubling we may find the recent electoral gains of the far-right, their relatively modest scale can be attributed to the comprehensive defeat suffered by their side in the 1970s and the tradition of militant anti-fascism that has continued to dog their efforts ever since. It is the experience of crushing defeat, rather than the arrival of Thatcherism, which best explains British fascism's subsequent failure to make the leap to nationwide electoral credibility that some of its European cousins have enjoyed.

RAR was an important partner in the anti-racist and anti-fascist mobilisations of the 1970s. The people who founded the movement felt they had an urgent task to perform and they seized on the opportunities that presented themselves at the time, and for doing so they deserve credit for setting an example of politico-cultural fusion that has acted as an inspiration for others. Notwithstanding certain critics, it seems that some revolutionaries *do* dance.

Notes

1 For a sustained critique of left-wing influence see Blake Baker, *The Far Left: An exposé of the extreme left in Britain* (Weidenfeld and Nicolson, London, 1981).

2 Ian Birchall cites the SWP's experience in the Vietnam Solidarity Campaign, where the tendency retained its room for manoeuvre and made significant

political gains by maintaining its critical and organisational independence of the movement's leadership. This was in contrast to the relatively poor performance of the International Marxist Group, which took a prominent leading role throughout the life of the campaign: Ian Birchall, interview (9 May 2001).

3 Caroline Coon, 'The Man Who Would Be Fuehrer' [sic], *Sounds* (25 March 1978), p. 31.

4 Gilroy, *There Ain't No Black*, pp. 115–117.

5 I am grateful to Ausaf Abbas for pointing out the strong 'Bollywood' references in Baz Luhrmann's *Moulin Rouge*; another instance of the growing influence of Asian style throughout the realm of popular culture.

6 Widgery, *Beating Time*, pp. 111–112.

Index

Note: page numbers in *italic* refer to illustrations, 'n.' after a page reference indicates the number of a note on that page.